Denise Schonwald is a remark[able]
one she works with. It has truly been a pleasure to get to know and
work with her and her clients. She is gifted in her healing abilities and
is generous in the help she provides to others. She is always helping
people around her to find ways to improve, and live a better happier
life. I highly recommend her services, and her book to all my clients,
friends and family.

—Anne Marie Doll
MHt, LC, RM, PC, SHA
Healing Life Center

I would highly recommend Denise for anyone looking to improve their life. She is more than my therapist; she is a life saver. She gave me the tools to take my life back.

—A. K.

A visit with Denise is as comfortable as having a conversation with an old friend. You will know from the beginning that she cares and wants you to live your best life every day.

—J. S.

I am a registered nurse and had the privilege to work with Denise in critical care for more years than I care to remember. She is gifted with a wonderful intellect as well as an empathetic and compassionate soul.

—E. O.

Denise Schonwald helped my daughter navigate through a very difficult family law situation. Denise developed such a rapport with my daughter that she still asks for a session from time to time. She is truly a blessing to my daughter and my family.

—L.K.

Bardolf & Company

HEALING YOUR BODY
BY MASTERING YOUR MIND

ISBN 978-1-938842-51-1
Copyright © 2020 by Denise Schonwald

Published by Bardolf & Company
www.bardolfandcompany.com

Cover design by *shawcreativegroup.com*
Jennifer Owen, Illustrator
Erica Ellis, Ink Deep Editing
Christine Nicole Photography for pictures of Denise
Devin Giles, photograph of Max

To my husband, Harvey

who is my dearest friend and colleague. He has supported me
in every aspect of my life, including parenting our children,
working all hours as a nurse, enrolling in graduate school,
writing a book, coaching me in tennis, and staying
out of my way while I was cleaning the house.

To my children and grandchildren

who are wonderful, strong, and independent.
They have all made us very proud.
We are grateful for our family and cherish them.

To my parents and my sisters

God bless the broken road that has taught me
to do my own work and to trust God to do the rest.

To my many friends and spirit guides

who support me and encourage me
to do more for the greater good. I thank you.

And to my therapy dog Max

who taught me many lessons while we practiced together
for most of his fifteen years.
This book was finally put to paper when I wanted
to honor his life by doing something memorable.
I am confident Henry will continue his legacy.

Healing Your Body
by
Mastering Your Mind

Denise Schonwald
BSRN, LMHC

Bardolf & Company
Sarasota, Florida

Contents

Denise Schonwald

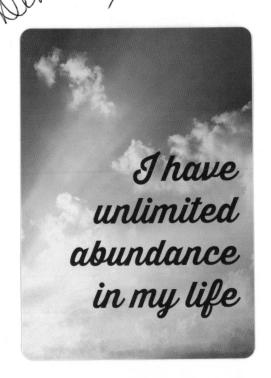

Introduction

I spent many years working as a nurse in the intensive care unit (ICU) and gained a great deal of understanding about the body. Seasoned ICU nurses must have excellent critical thinking skills that allow them to interpret the body's symptoms and understand its messages. We saved many lives by reacting quickly. Some crises were prevented by interpreting objective medical data, while others were prevented by acting purely on a gut instinct. It was an honor to work with a great group of intelligent and compassionate nurses. I learned so much following their lead.

But I have always loved psychology. Although I enjoyed the intellectual challenges of nursing, I enjoyed the deeper connection with the person behind the monitor even more. I worked nights most of my career in the ICU for this reason. Shortly after I'd start my shift at 7:00 p.m., the doctors would go home (hopefully) and the unit would get quiet. I always bathed my patients even though we had nursing techs who would offer to do it. For me, it was the best time to listen to and learn from the body: the temperature of the patient's skin, the color of their legs, how well their wounds were healing. It took at least an hour, and I enjoyed getting to know my patients, even when they were too weak to have a conversation with me. The body has a way of communicating without words. It is called energy. Since as far back as I can remember, I have had the ability to understand and know things about people just by interpreting their energy or, to put it simply, "feeling their vibe." Trust me, sometimes I wish I couldn't. The struggle throughout the years was trusting it or perhaps being mature enough to use it wisely.

My husband once described psychology as a soft science and, at the time, I couldn't argue with him. A soft science is one that doesn't provide hard objective measures to help form a diagnosis. For example, why is someone anxious? Stress? Childhood issues? Past trauma? How are we describing anxiety? Nervousness? Obsessive-compulsiveness? Overthinking? Perfectionism? Pleasing? Maybe this is the reason why many people ignore their anxiety or live with their depression. I wonder if it would make a difference if people knew a great number of physical problems were the result of psychological problems and vice versa? It is a connection many people fail to realize. I hope after you finish reading this book, you will understand this connection better.

The body needs to maintain balance in order to stay healthy. It has the ability to correct itself without relying on us to do anything to help it. Have you ever had a teeth chattering chill which raised your temperature because of an infection? Once this passed, you suddenly felt hot, started sweating, and your temperature returned to normal. What happened? The body automatically corrected the imbalance. In medicine, we call it homeostasis.

Psychologically speaking, a person needs to balance between his sympathetic nervous system and his parasympathetic nervous system. Our sympathetic nervous system is activated when the body has a sudden, involuntary response to danger or a situation it perceives as stressful. The body will automatically respond to these types of events with increased focus, elevated heart rate, while sending extra blood to our muscles to signal our "fight or flight" response. We spend lots of time in our sympathetic nervous system: work, running errands, answering emails, sending texts, making phone calls, day to day stress, you name it. The parasympathetic nervous system is active when the body is resting and replenishing, such as during digestion or when we relax. When this occurs, the heart rate slows down. This is when we are simply "being." We frequently don't make time (not find time, make time) for those activities that bring us into our parasympathetic nervous system as much as we should. An easy way to remember the difference is sympathetic is doing and parasympathetic is being. Parasympathetic activities are things like reading, listening to music, going to the beach, playing an instrument, knitting, yoga, fishing, enjoying a hobby, playing a sport—whatever brings your heart joy.

When the body is not in balance, it will require ease. If we don't choose appropriate ways to cope with stress, balancing sympathetic and parasympathetic, it is likely for an addiction to creep its way into our lives. Alcohol, cigarettes, spending, watching pornography, overeating, and getting high are things we rely on in order to find ease, but the consequences of these choices can be dire. They can cost us our relationships, our livelihoods, and maybe even our lives.

After graduating from Nova Southeastern University, I went into my internship with confidence and spent time with a lot of therapists. Many typed into their tablet during the session, taking copious notes in one hour, which I figured would be helpful in order to keep everyone's problems and issues straight. It seemed efficient but was definitely not for me. I knew I couldn't type and pay attention at the same time. So I decided to rely on my memory. Sounds easy enough except for the fact I was going to see thousands of clients, and my brain could only hold so much. Yet remembering each case came fairly easily for me. When I was new in practice and seeing six to eight clients a week, I would go back to the previous week and quiz myself. It amazed me how much I could remember about each client: Jill is married to John, her father-in-law passed away suddenly, and their son is struggling with substance abuse. When I was reviewing my patients' problems in my mind, it occurred to me that those with the same physical problems had the same psychological problems.

That day was the beginning of the incredible journey I have been on ever since. I started by looking more deeply into the body for insight. I studied with a Shaman, explored many religions, learned hypnosis, read dozens of books, became a master of Reiki, and began practicing yoga. What I discovered, over my many years of research, was a fascinating way of helping patients learn to interpret this energy in order to heal themselves. This is the foundation for how I practice psychology.

This book will start by explaining internal energy, where it is located, what parts of the body it affects, and what emotional and spiritual components it addresses. We will move on to talk about what happens when these energies are blocked, both physically and emotionally. You will learn and practice techniques and methods I have learned to increase the flow of energy and unblock the chakras. There are many ways to unblock energy, and I will describe a few after each chapter to give you some suggestions. I hope you will continue to do more research on your own. Lastly, I am going to share my personal journey with energy as well as case studies I have seen in private practice.

Please consider reading this book from start to finish with an open mind, an open heart, and an open spirit. I don't expect you to take my word because you know me or because I have written it. I do, however, hope you will begin to do your own work and simply be open to looking at the world, your life, and your body a little differently. You may notice God is mentioned in almost every chapter, which may be challenging if you are not religious. I understand many have different beliefs and values, and I honor your choice regardless of what it is. If God is not something or someone you believe in, I'm asking you to, instead, trust the energy of the Universe for answers and wisdom. This is our intuition, these are our "God whispers," as Oprah calls it.[1] This is that little voice in the back of our head that offers guidance when we least expect it.

As you continue reading, you may begin to realize you are more familiar with energy than you thought. My goal is to bring it all together to give you the tools to heal from within. I hope, by reading this book, you can learn to trust your body; learn to forgive, grieve, correct, and grow; and move forward to a wonderful life of peace and happiness. You deserve it.

Denise Schonwald
Sarasota, Florida, 2020

---

[1] "Pay Attention to the Whispers of the Universe," Oprah Winfrey, uploaded 3/9/18 by OWN, https://www.youtube.com/watch?v=22bSDShY9LI

Chapter 1

The Energy Within

Understanding Internal Energy

Everything in our world is made up of energy. Most of us began learning about the energy of the outside world in school when we were in science class. We frequently don't appreciate energy and how much we rely on it until we are without it. There is nothing like a two-day power outage to help us realize how much we take energy for granted.

There is also an internal energy, the energy within our body. As you read through each chapter, gaining a clearer understanding of the body and emotions along the way, try to envision the energy connected to the emotion discussed. For example, anxiety is too much energy in the body, while depression is not enough. Emotions have a vibrational frequency, an electrical charge, if you will. Negative emotions have a low vibrational frequency while positive emotions have a higher one.

Have you ever thought about the power of energy? Think about things you have heard people say, such as "Put your mind to it," "Be careful what you wish for," "Where there's a will there's a way," and "Focus!" Energy flows where it is directed. I learned about the power of energy working in the ICU. I took care of an elderly woman who wanted to see her son before she died. She knew she was dying. Her heart rate was 35 beats per minute (normal is 60–100 beats per minute) when I told her that her son had just landed at the airport. It would be another hour before he could get to the hospital to see her, and she was barely conscious when I told her he was on his way. I remember thinking, "She'll never make it." Suddenly, her heart rate increased to 60 beats per minute, and she rallied until her son walked into the room. He lowered his head next to hers and whispered in his mother's ear, "Mom, I'm here." She looked up at him, smiled, and she died.

I saw many cases like this, and I learned to never underestimate the power of our will, the mind, and its energy. I began to focus my own energy more positively through visualization, goal setting, mindfulness, creating a vision board, and, most importantly, through prayer. I learned to practice gratefulness through sad times and to visualize a happier ending even if I had trouble believing it myself. I can't say it was always easy, but I trusted the process. It is called faith.

The Power of Negative Energy

Have you ever felt very depressed? If you have, you probably barely had enough energy to brush your teeth, take a shower, or even eat a simple meal. I can remember a time in high school when my first boyfriend broke up with me, and I had to call my mom to pick me up from school early because I could barely function. (On the flip side, I could stay up half the night talking to my teammates when we were traveling to play basketball. I can remember not feeling a bit tired at 2:30 a.m., even though we had to play in a tournament the following day.) Anxiety and anger are also low energies. While anxiety and anger may appear to be high-vibrational energies, because they are intense emotions, their frequencies are actually low. Anxiety and anger are very stressful on the heart.

I remember, even as a child, feeling a knot in the pit of my stomach when someone betrayed my trust. I didn't realize until years later that it was energy blocking around my stomach. I think we have all had that feeling of unbearable, immense pain in our heart after losing someone we loved, not understanding the fact that energy was blocking around the heart.

Negative thinkers, pessimists, complainers, and overly dramatic people have a buildup of negative emotions in the body. These emotions are energy pullers, meaning energy is directed toward the negativity. This is the reason why you may have felt exhausted after being around someone who constantly complains. Both an anxious person and a depressed person pull energy toward themselves. Both energies can be overwhelming to be around.

It is important for us to realize that we can learn how to control our emotions as well as the way we perceive events and circumstances. We can learn to use negative energies as agents for growth. Or we can choose to use negative energy to create fear or justify our egos. The ego thinks our thoughts and opinions are more important or more valuable than anyone else's. We feel our way is the only way and things cannot be done right if we aren't involved. This type of energy is controlling, pretentious, and self-centered, which causes the energy to pull and focus on the self. My friend David liked to call these individuals very "special" people.

The Power of Positive Energy

On a more positive note, people who are happy, joyful, grateful, and peaceful will emit positive, higher-vibrational energies to everyone they meet. These are the people you love to be around. They are the characters in the movies or in storybooks that make us smile just by looking at their faces. There are people in my life who are a joy to spend time with. I love how happy they are, how great I feel when I am around them, and I never get tired of being in their company. Even when these people are going through hard times, they handle it calmly, with positivity and grace. What a wonderful way to go through life.

Reframing—changing the way you view your experiences and emotions—is an effective tool to help increase vibrational energy. I practice reframing on a daily basis. I never realized how much I needed it until I started noticing my negative thought patterns. I can remember drinking my coffee in the morning and thinking, "This is going to be the worst day ever!" It certainly was going to be a long day, but thinking it was going to be the worst day was my way of catastrophizing. I started asking myself how I knew this to be true, especially since I was still in my pajamas. Now I think about my long days ahead and say things like, "Today is going to be a busy day, but I am looking forward to a nice walk and a hot bath when I get home."

We can also increase our vibrational energy by letting go of our ego. Tough one, I know. Every morning, I ask God and the Universe for the courage to speak up when I need to or to use my voice for those who are unable to speak for themselves. I also ask for wisdom to know when to be quiet and listen, the time when no words are needed. This daily practice has helped me resist offering my opinion (particularly when no one has asked me for it), resorting to sarcasm, and, most importantly, pointing out my husband's character flaws. It is a courtesy I'm sure he has extended to his darling wife a time or two.

A gratitude journal is one of the easiest and most effective ways to generate positivity. I have found it extremely beneficial when I'm going through tough times. Practicing gratitude has helped shift the focus because it is nearly impossible to be positive and negative at the same time. I start my day speaking (out loud) all the things I'm grateful for. I have quite the list.

Energy of Children

Energy fluctuations can be more noticeable in children than adults. Kids can be very happy one minute and then very sad the next. Something as simple as offering ice cream to a crying child can create a positive energy shift. Children are very sensitive to energy, which explains why they typically misbehave when there is tension or stress in the home. Parents tell me, "We never argue in front of the children," but the truth is kids pick up on their hostile energy regardless of whether their parents fight in front of them or not.

When children come to my office for counseling, it is usually because of some sort of behavioral problem. After ruling out a learning or developmental delay, I typically ask the parent, "How do they behave at school?" If the child has no problems behaving appropriately at school, the problem is usually within the family system. I have found when I approach the parents with my concerns, it is likely the last time I will see their child in my office. It can be painful to look within and take ownership of our weaknesses. Some parents are unable to look in the mirror for fear of what they may see. It can be frightening. I have looked but it wasn't as bad as my mind had imagined it to be.

In our world today, kids are having problems regulating energy because they are using too much technology. I see young children with anger issues, depression, severe anxiety, and many who are socially awkward. Their legs bounce incessantly during session, energy bursting through their limbs, trying to get out of their body. I have had more than one child tell me their dream job would be to play video games or be a YouTuber.

When I was a child, we spent more time outside than we did inside. We played tag, hide and seek, and badminton, and ran around our neighborhood until our parents called us home because it was getting dark. We got rid of a lot of physical energy, and we learned to use our imaginations to be creative when we were bored. Today, kids are hibernating in their bedrooms watching YouTube and playing video games that are not age appropriate. Since I started in private practice, I've had three patients who were very tempted to take a swing at me. All three were young boys who were angry with me for telling their parents to limit their screen time. Their reaction only reinforced the severity of the problem. Those parents who took my advice saw a huge turnaround in their child's behavior. Those who did not have the courage to tackle the issue left my office and will ultimately have bigger problems down the road. I have no doubt about it.

The Anatomy of Chakras

In order to gain a better understanding of the energy centers in the body, where they are located and what they do, **let's look at the diagram on the next page.** The dots running through the midline of a person's body are concentrated energy centers known as chakras. Many people have no idea these energies even exist.

The term "chakras" comes from the Sanskrit word for wheel or disc. The Chinese call the same energy chi; yogis refer to this energy as Shakti. I like to think of these energies as energetic "gates" that will open and close depending on our emotions, feelings, circumstances, and experiences. Lack of energy flow will provide an ideal "host" for illness.

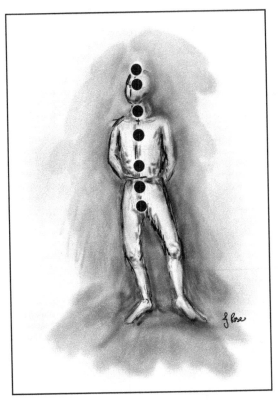

I will be referring to each energetic gate using the word chakra. My Christian upbringing taught me it was not Godly to study chakras. I still have no idea why. For me, learning about energy has deepened my faith in God, and I am more spiritual now than ever.

The circle at the bottom of the diagram, at the base of the spine, is our grounding chakra, which we will discuss in more detail in the next chapter. This is the energetic field that forms our foundation. When it is blocked, we are not at peace, we have difficulty standing up for ourselves, we feel uncomfortable in our own skin. Blockage in this chakra is apparent when we fail to set boundaries, we are people pleasers, we rescue others, we are condescending, we yell, we overthink. Physically, people who have blocked root chakras can suffer from back pain, rectal tumors, depression, fibromyalgia, lupus, MS, and other autoimmune disorders.

The next circle, above the grounding chakra, is below the stomach but above the base of the spine over our pelvic region. The energies within this chakra are associated with blame, guilt, money, control, sex, and creativity. Blockages in the second chakra are manifested by infertility, lack of libido, irregular menstruation, bowel problems, urinary problems, and back pain.

The third circle is located over the abdomen. Emotions within this energy are truth, fear, self-esteem, sensitivity to criticism, self-respect, and self-care. Blockages here (solar plexus) will cause people to overeat, not eat, drink too much alcohol, and manifest physically with arthritis, eating disorders, bowel problems, diabetes, indigestion, and liver problems.

The fourth circle is right over our heart. It is vital to understand this one, as our hearts are what we open to connect to each other. Here we hold emotions like love, hatred, bitterness, resentment, grief, hope, loneliness, forgiveness, compassion, anger, anxiety. Physically, many with energy blockages of their heart can suffer from lung cancer, breast cancer, and heart and lung problems, including asthma and allergies. People blocked at the heart for long periods of time are likely to smoke. When they inhale and exhale cigarette smoke, the chakra will open and the energy will flow. People who smoke say it relaxes them or helps them deal with stress and anxiety. Unfortunately, the chakra is opened by choosing something harmful.

The fifth circle is over our throat. This is the chakra connected to using our voice to express ourselves, faith, following our dreams, and personal expression. It is also connected to addiction When the throat chakra is blocked, many suffer from thyroid problems, raspy throat, mouth ulcers, TMJ, chronic laryngitis, and so on.

The sixth circle, often called the third eye, is our intelligence. For the most part, we are fairly intelligent beings, and I have only seen this chakra closed when patients have had a developmental disability or in very close-minded individuals. As you can imagine, close-minded individuals rarely come in for therapy and, when they do, it can make for a long hour in session.

The chakra at the top of the head is our spiritual energy, the energy that connects us to God or the Universe, our higher power, something or someone greater than ourselves. It is this chakra that opens when we practice humanitarianism, spirituality, and selflessness and allows us to trust life and trust God and to see the bigger picture. It is the God whisper we hear when we ask. I rely on this energetic gate to be open in order to help me counsel people. It is amazing and unnerving at the same time to feel the energy flow of this chakra and listen to your intuition. I have learned to trust it even when I am not sure where it is leading me. Energy will communicate to you, too; you just need to understand its language.

Before you continue reading any further, I want to be clear about my intention for writing this book. I will be sharing an accounting of what I have learned about energy and how I use it to help people heal. While I am clear in my own beliefs and values, I would never want to offend, disrespect, or disregard the beliefs and values of others. This book is my story, my journey, and what I know to be true. I have been educated and have practiced medicine and/or psychology for nearly thirty years. I have a strong spiritual connection, and I have combined all of these modalities to help others. The knowledge I am sharing with you comes straight from my heart.

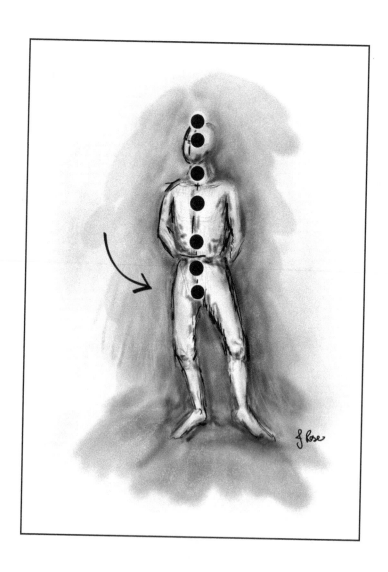

Chapter 2

The First Chakra:
The Root Chakra—
A Sturdy Foundation

Understanding This Energy

This energetic field is located at the base of the spine. I like to call it our grounding chakra, the energy that flows at our foundation and evolves from the beliefs and values of our family. Some refer to this energy as our tribal energy. Take a minute to visualize this area of the body as we discuss what organs or parts of the body are affected in this area. Located in the root chakra is the base of the spine, which is what supports our body physically (bones, legs, feet). The rectum is also in this area.

The root chakra is our foundation and a sturdy foundation normally develops in childhood. We rely on our parents and extended family to teach us the rules of society and how to take care of ourselves, hopefully offering a lot of love and support along the way. If you were fortunate enough to have parents like this, you are envied by many people.

When our root chakra is open, energy is flowing, and we feel at peace. We learn to provide for ourselves and we feel at home, not only in our physical house but within ourselves. If we have grown up in a dysfunctional home, where we were exposed to addiction, violence, abuse, or mental illness, this energy gate may remain closed for long periods of time.

What Causes the Root Chakra to Close and Block Energy?

With the majority of clients I see blocked in this area, the root chakra has been blocked since childhood. It can be tough for children who have grown up in a dysfunctional household where there is abuse and addiction to overcome. When children have not been raised on a firm foundation, where they feel loved, safe, and at peace, the root chakra blocks energy. Some of the stories I have heard were just heartbreaking.

Many children who grow up in this type of environment repeat the cycle. After living many years of heartache and suffering, they eventually grow up, move out of their toxic and dysfunctional home, and get right back into another toxic relationship. Many of these children later develop a personality disorder known as "dependent personality," where they lack the ability to make decisions on their own, allow others to treat them inappropriately, rely on and need constant approval from others, and are often physically, emotionally, and sexually abused as adults. These adult personality disorders are the most challenging to work with because this relationship dynamic, although extremely inappropriate and unacceptable, is what they have known their entire lives as "normal."

Blockages do not always start in childhood. It is possible patients may have had a wonderful childhood but now find themselves in an unhappy marriage. Unresolved trauma can also cause grounding energy to block if not addressed. Traumas are often sudden, unexpected, and unprepared for. A trauma can turn our world upside down.

Even when traumas are anticipated, perhaps the death of someone battling a terminal illness, the root chakra can still block after a loved one passes. It has been my experience that a person who has been fairly healthy psychologically before a trauma will eventually find a "new" normal and recover. Those who had suffered from other psychological stressors before a traumatic event may not recover as easily. This is typically known as post-traumatic stress disorder (PTSD).

If we think about it honestly, there have been times we have all handled stress or conflict inappropriately. Whether it happened once in a while or became a pattern, the behavior stemmed from energy that was blocked at the root chakra.

When counseling a client with a block at the root chakra, I present them with the following examples of ways to handle conflict and stress and ask them if they relate to any of them. I am able to gain valuable information based on their reaction. I used animals for each one to provide a quick visualization for easy reference.

Which ones do you connect with?

1. The Erupter

This is a person who may not yell or call names but will become easily irritated or annoyed when frustrated, overwhelmed, or disappointed. If you are not an erupter, you have probably met one. If not, go to the grocery store and stand by the customer service counter. You will likely see this type of person in action.

The erupter has difficulty expressing his emotions without an excessive amount of energy. This is very strenuous on the heart. After an outburst, the erupter will likely be filled with remorse because he has said things he wished he had not said or acted in a way he wished he had not but, unfortunately, the damage has been done.

2. The Concealer

The concealer will not speak up and refuses to talk about a conflict. It can be a mystery to know what she is thinking. You might even ask the concealer, "Are you okay?" and she will say "yes" even though you are fairly certain she means "no." Many concealers struggle with depression because they store these unresolved and unhappy feelings in their body.

Negative feelings that stay in the body and may lead to depression include feeling unimportant, not being appreciated, insecurity, unresolved hurt and pain, and guilt. I am sure there are many more.

QUESTION: What happens when the erupter meets the concealer?

ANSWER: They get married!

This is because the erupter and the concealer make a good pair based on the way they handle problems, even if the fit is dysfunctional. Neither one helps the other learn to resolve conflict appropriately. Have you met this couple? I am betting so!

3. The Alarmist

You all have met this person. This person does not know how to address a problem with the person he has concerns with. Instead, he will tell everyone who will give him an opportunity to vent. Social media provides the ideal platform for an alarmist. The alarmist may think he is justified in ranting on Facebook about his frustrations, but this reaction is actually inappropriate and emotionally immature.

There is nothing wrong with talking to someone about a problem and asking for advice. Catharsis, the term we use in psychology to mean to release strong emotions or simply vent, can be therapeutic and healing. The difference is the alarmist never addresses the problem with the person directly in order to resolve the issue. Running a thought, concern, or idea by someone for the purpose of seeking direction on how to handle it is perfectly acceptable as long as it is done appropriately. A counselor can provide helpful insight.

4. The Slitherer

It is not unusual or even abnormal for kids to try to worm or slither out of trouble. Kids say things like "not my fault" or "he did it first, so punish him." As children grow older, parents should help them learn to take responsibility for their choices or actions. Helpful words are "I understand you are disappointed you can't go out and play but whose responsibility was it to take out the garbage?" They may not like the questions, but learning to take responsibility and be accountable for our actions are crucial lessons we can teach our children to help them develop emotional maturity and integrity.

Unfortunately, many people grow into adulthood never learning to take responsibility for their actions. We call their parents "enablers," "rescuers," "helicopter parents," or even "neglectful." When their children grow up, they blame other people for things they don't like, don't have, don't want, or are unwilling to take responsibility for.

5. The Accommodator

The accommodator, sometimes referred to as a pleaser, will settle for any solution as long as it pleases the other person. She will say "yes" when she means "no" and "no" when she means "yes."

Emily Maroutian gave some great insight into people pleasers in her wonderful book, *The Energy of Emotions*:

> *People-pleasing doesn't work very long because it's a conditional energy and can shift in a moment. We either end up exhausting ourselves trying to please everyone or we open ourselves up for being used.*
>
> *People-pleasing is a form of manipulation, because we attempt to control how others feel, even if we are trying to make them feel good. We want to alter the conditions around us so we can create better energy within us. We want other people to act better so we can feel better when we look at them. We place the responsibility of our feelings on other people. We may want them to feel good or receive some kind of benefit as well, but it's ultimately about our own anxieties in need of relief.*[1]

The pleaser has a lot of challenges. It is impossible to please everyone all the time, which can be extremely frustrating for the pleaser. The pleaser also has poorly defined boundaries. Boundaries define who we are as individuals. They are what separates us from someone else. If we have poorly defined boundaries, we are susceptible to being manipulated, abused, cheated, or taken advantage of.

Signs of Unhealthy Boundaries

Telling everything.

Disclosing at an intimate level early in a relationship.

Falling in love with someone you just met.

Feeling responsible for helping anyone who reaches out.

---

[1] Emily Maroutian, *The Energy of Emotions: The 10 Emotional Environments and How They Shape the World Around Us* (United States CreateSpace Independent Publishing Platform, 2015).

Being preoccupied with another person.

Acting on the first sexual impulse.

Being sexual for your partner, not yourself.

Going against personal values or rights to please another.

Rationalizing or not noticing another person who displays inappropriate boundaries or invades your boundaries.

Accepting and tolerating physical responses you don't want.

Touching a person without asking.

Giving as much as you can for the sake of giving.

Allowing someone to take as much as he can from you.

Letting others direct your life.

Letting others describe your reality.

Letting others define you.

Believing others can anticipate your needs.

Falling apart so that someone will take care of you.

Self-abuse.[2]

When we dishonor ourselves because of poorly defined boundaries, excess negative energy builds up in the body, which will need to be released. Often, it comes out in the form of addiction or through what I refer to as a "lovey." A lovey is something inappropriate we go to in order to give the body ease such as gambling, overeating, yelling, smoking, drinking, spending, or pornography. These coping mechanisms can develop into addictions if we are not mindful.

---

[2] "Signs of Unhealthy Boundaries," Healing Private Wounds, https://www.healingprivatewounds.org/wp-content/uploads/2014/04/week_5b_boundaries.pdf

6. The File Clerk

The file clerk is very similar to the concealer. The difference is that when the file clerk finally speaks up, he will likely have a library of ammunition to justify his feelings. With this arsenal of weaponry, it is likely for the file clerk to become an erupter, again, saying and doing things he later regrets.

When we don't feel comfortable within ourselves, we are not grounded. When our lives at home are chaotic, we cannot feel at peace. When we block energy at our foundation, it is no coincidence that we eventually get sick.

The Physical or Psychological Effect of Blocked Energy at the First Chakra

Depression manifests from blocking at the root chakra. Depression occurs when we have persistent feelings of sadness and other low-vibrational energies such as shame, loneliness, worthlessness, and emptiness.

These deep-seated feelings get stored in our subconscious mind. To better understand our levels of awareness, let's take a moment to review them:

We have three levels of awareness.

The first one is our UNCONSCIOUS awareness. We love this one. It is the state we are in when we are going about our day and not having to think about what we are doing. Have you ever driven somewhere and have no memory of how you got there? This is what I'm referring to, and this is why we love routine.

The second level of awareness is our CONSCIOUS awareness. This level of awareness requires us to think about what we are doing. We often don't like this one. This is why we don't like to change habits (even ones we don't like), stay on a diet, or start a new job.

The last level of awareness is our SUBCONSCIOUS awareness. Subconscious describes something that is below our thinking mind. The cells and the organs in our body have an awareness that sometimes the conscious mind cannot remember. Think about all the experiences you have had throughout your life. We don't remember most of them, and they passed right through our bodies. However, some experiences or our perception of the experience left us feeling inferior, ashamed, humiliated, and so one. These thoughts sit in our subconscious and will come to the surface and cloud a new experience even if the original experience occurred back in our childhood.

For example: A parent verbally abuses his child, humiliates him, calls him names, and makes him feel ashamed and worthless. These feelings become stored in the body, sometimes for decades, and will infiltrate his everyday life one way or another. An everyday experience, such as a remark by a stranger, will be tainted negatively for a depressed person, whereas a healthier person could have the exact same experience and think nothing of it.

Back pain is another symptom of blocked energy in the root chakra. When a client comes into my office and puts the pillow from my sofa behind his back, I tune into the grounding chakra. You may be thinking, maybe he was in an accident. Maybe he has some sort of congenital back problem. I agree; right now I am just noticing. When a patient has a history of fibromyalgia, I also focus my questions around the root chakra.

Autoimmune disorders, rectal tumors, and rectal cancer are other illnesses I have seen develop when this chakra is blocked. An autoimmune disorder occurs when the body fights against itself, manifesting disorders such as lupus, fibromyalgia, celiac disease, rheumatoid arthritis, multiple sclerosis, psoriasis, and so on. It never ceases to amaze me how the energy connects. I have never known it to be inaccurate.

My Story

Looking back, I know there were many circumstances that affected my root chakra. My sisters and I grew up with a father who suffered from bipolar disorder. His emotions and behaviors were erratic and unpredictable when he was unstable. Medication can be very helpful for a person struggling with bipolar depression but, many times, a person with bipolar will stop taking his medication when he feels stable. This was our father. The "highs" were high and the "lows" were dark. Our mother wasn't equipped to handle him, and our lives at home were not always peaceful.

I could feel both my parents' energies in my body. I could tell when things were good and when things were about to get ugly. One look at my father could cause my grounding chakra to close. My mother would say he was having a "spell," and his face had an expression I can still recognize in old photographs.

My childhood wasn't always unhappy and my grounding chakra wasn't always closed; we had happy times too. Our mother was very active in our church, and her faith in God helped us find some stability in life. I felt peace in church and there were many people in our congregation I looked up to. We would sing hymns, and I would literally feel my chakras open, particularly my heart. I went to a Christian school, and I was surrounded by many teachers who helped me feel grounded. Although the school was tough academically, I felt my feet standing on a firm foundation surrounded by many who cared about me. I felt it in their energy. Our grandparents were pretty special too.

Aside from church, I found other ways to feel grounded and at peace. I loved playing with dolls. I once heard someone say she would never let their daughter have a Barbie doll because girls should not feel pressured to look like Barbie: tall, skinny, big busted, with blonde hair. But Barbie helped introduce me to my friend up the street. She not only had a Ken doll, she had a Barbie camper. We played for hours with those dolls. Barbie and Ken were happy together. My friend was biracial and chubby. I was chubby, too, with crooked teeth and tangled hair. Neither of us wanted to look like Barbie. We just wanted to have fun. I guess everything in life comes down to perspective.

As I mentioned earlier, recovering from an unhappy or unstable childhood takes work. The story I told about my parents is not the story I hold in my body. I know my parents did the best they could with the skills they had. They didn't try to harm us; they had unresolved issues that had nothing to do with us. I forgave them. I harbor no bitterness or resentment, but I also did the work to heal.

Some people never recover from those early feelings of not feeling loved or valued. It is unfortunate to see behaviors and patterns travel down from generation to generation. Unresolved issues and problems will not be resolved unless the person is willing to do the work needed in order to heal. A trained professional can help a person change old habits, thoughts, and behaviors and build healthier ones. This is when life begins to feel more beautiful.

Case Study

I had a lovely woman in her fifties call me asking if I accepted new clients. She and her husband wanted to come for marriage counseling, and she hoped I could work around their busy work schedule. We came up with a time that worked for all of us, and they came in a few days later. The woman was poised, quiet, and reserved. Her husband was a narcissist. I could feel his energy when he walked into my office and knew it was going to be a tough session. He answered my questions in an ever-so-slightly condescending manner while she sat quietly with a glazed look on her face. She only spoke when I asked her questions, but he was quick to chime in and take over. He was animated, loud, and obnoxious. When I asked them if there was any history of abuse, the wife said she was raised in an extremely abusive household and had been physically, emotionally, and sexually abused as a young girl. She, like many others I have seen throughout the years, grew up and partnered with a narcissist. Her husband felt she should be happy because he provided her a home and made a nice income. He put her down in front of their children, he pointed at her in session, he was mean, he was abusive. She said she kept hoping he would change.

Both these clients, husband and wife, are blocked at the root chakra. Narcissists are insecure, which is why they have an over-inflated opinion of themselves. The husband had a history of back pain, leg pain, spinal abnormalities, and fibromyalgia. His wife barely spoke in session. Her voice was so soft, I had a hard time understanding her. She said her friends and family would be shocked if their marriage didn't survive. I could not imagine it to be true.

Will this couple stay together? Yes, likely they will, but they will probably not come back to therapy. After our initial visit, the husband left very upset, which made the wife feel guilty. She wanted me to reassure her the marriage was worth saving because she had invested over a decade of her life with this man. It was all I could do to make it through an hour with him. After I saw this couple for a few weeks, I got a text from the wife late on a Friday night saying, "Thank you for your help, Denise, but we have decided not to continue with any more sessions with you."

It is difficult to handle stress and conflict appropriately when the root chakra is blocked. In this case, the husband used anger and intimidation when he didn't get his way. His wife hid her feelings and remained hopeful therapy would help them. I have no doubt they are still together.

How to Open the Root Chakra

Again, this is our foundation. If there is no inner peace in the body, the work needs to be done to restore energy flow to this area.

Counseling: Believe it or not, fear prevents people from coming to therapy. The thought of looking behind the dark corners of our lives can be frightening. Yet, it is impossible to heal if these areas are not addressed.

Before choosing a therapist, please do your homework and find someone licensed with the proper credentials. You wouldn't pick a physician who had been to a two-week seminar taught by a renowned doctor and had come home with a certificate to practice. I hope not, anyway. I have had four years of undergraduate school, a BS in nursing, three years of graduate school at a university (not online), and two years of internship, with one of those years working with substance abuse. After my internship, I took two sets of boards, one to practice in the state of Florida and the other to practice nationally. You owe it to yourself to find someone licensed and competent to help you heal. Insist this person has the proper training.

Iyanla Vanzant said that in order to do the work, you need to "feel it, deal with it, and heal from it."[3] Counseling is something people can incorporate into their lives even if they don't go on a regular basis. There are situations that happen in my life when I know I need to make an appointment with my therapist. However, a therapist is just one tool. In order to stay mentally healthy, you need a toolbox. I have a super-sized one.

Hypnosis: No, a hypnotherapist is not going to put you to sleep and make you cluck like a chicken or bark like a dog. I cannot tell you how many patients have these types of concerns. A trained hypnotherapist can help a person combat phobias, break bad habits, decrease stress, decrease chronic pain, boost self-confidence,

---

[3] "Iyanla Vanzant Defines Pain," Iyanla Vanzant, uploaded 3/18/12 by OWN https://www.youtube.com/watch?v=xk6DTEK02CE

increase sports performance, fight fatigue and insomnia, and more. I average a session every few months. Hypnosis is one of the most powerful tools in my toolbox. I have many to help keep me balanced.

Daily grounding/prayer: Grounding or prayer is a good way to start the day by focusing energy in a positive direction. For many who pray routinely, the root chakra opens when they connect to God.

Every morning, I spend time grounding. I begin by practicing gratefulness and speak, out loud, the things I am thankful for. I am thankful for my gifts, talents, and abilities. I always ask for help using them to help others heal and do all that I do for the greater good. I trust God and the Universe to guide me, which helps me push through fear. I lift up those in need of light, love, healing, and ease. My list keeps getting longer and longer. I include my nephew, Nick, who is in remission from lymphoma; my college girlfriend, Edwina; and high school friend, Paul, also in remission from lymphoma. So many others I know and name. I also have a longer list of those who are grieving—my friends who have lost children or spouses, and my patients. If we really stop and think about it, we would be kinder and more compassionate knowing so many are suffering. We cannot escape pain and suffering, unfortunately, regardless of how much money we have or how well we behave.

Forgiveness: The root chakra opens when we offer forgiveness. While we don't understand things that have happened to us in the past, doing the work to heal allows us to process our past differently and heal. Setting an intention for healing, forgiveness, and understanding permits acceptance and willingness. Maybe we can forgive our mother or our father, who were never taught how to be a good parent, others who haven't done their own work and hurt us, or those who disappointed and betrayed our trust or abused us. I like Oprah's definition of forgiveness when she said, "Forgiveness is giving up the hope that the past could have been different."[4] Forgiving and accepting can help the root chakra open. It will also help you feel more at peace.

There are many other practices to help open the root chakra. A few of them include Reiki, meditation, yoga, spending time in nature, listening to peaceful music, attending a religious service, and aromatherapy.

A good way of helping our energy to flow at our foundation is to follow guidelines that help ground us. For me, it is the Ten Indian Commandments. I have a large poster of these commandments hanging in my garage right next to the door entering our home. If you take these commandments into your heart, they can help you too. I pray you can learn to honor yourself and help make our world a better place just by taking care of yourself and incorporating these guidelines into your life. We can never be helpful to others if we don't start by helping ourselves.

The Ten Indian Commandments

Remain close to great spirit.
Show great respect for your fellow beings.
Give assistance and kindness wherever needed.
Be truthful and honest at all times.
Do what you know to be right.
Look after the well-being of mind and body.

---

[4] "Oprah's Favorite Definition of Forgiveness," Oprah Winfrey, uploaded 3/15/18 by OWN

Treat the earth and all that dwell thereon with respect.
Take full responsibility for your actions.
Dedicate a share of your efforts to the greater good.
Work together for the benefit of all mankind.[5]

It is no coincidence that so many religions and philosophies preach the same guidance.

---

[5] https://www.youtube.com/watch?v=y-7p4gfVt6w

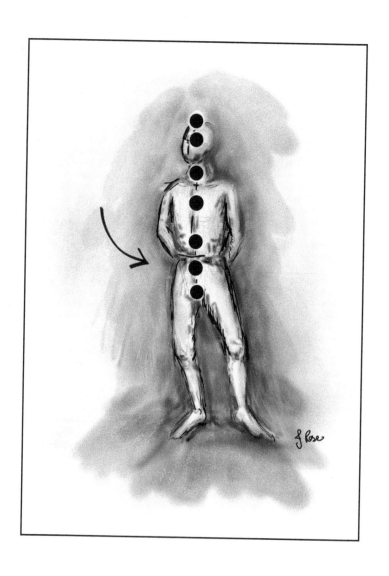

Chapter 3

The Second Chakra
The Sacral Chakra—
The Power behind
Forming Relationships

Understanding This Energy

The second chakra is located above the spine but below the abdomen. It sits on top of our sexual organs, intestines, lower back, bladder, and hips. This energy connects us personally to others through relationships. Our root chakra is our foundation, highly influenced by our upbringing, but the second chakra is associated with others outside our family or our tribe. This chakra begins to show an increase in energy flow around the age of seven or eight when children begin to explore their relationships with others, making choices of their own. Our connection to the environment is developing also. This includes our relationship with money, sexual experiences, personal power, fear of losing control, our ability to creatively express ourselves, and ethics and honor in relationships, not only with each other but also within ourselves. Many emotions contribute to the energy flow of the second chakra.

Blame and guilt are associated with this energy. Blame and guilt are emotions we frequently assign to ourselves inappropriately. We have had guests in our home insist on doing the dinner dishes, blaming it on "Catholic guilt." Another friend of ours chimed in and insisted "Jewish guilt" was worse than Catholic because Jewish people include the relatives for reinforcement to lay on the guilt. All kidding aside, guilt and blame are fear-based, low-vibrational energies that do not serve the body in a healthy way. To be clear, it is considerate and very polite to offer help with the dishes in another person's home. This should not be an offer stemming from fear.

There are times we have offended someone, hurt his feelings, and hopefully felt guilty about it later on. Guilt is felt when the second chakra closes and may result in gastrointestinal upset. If this is the case, by all means apologize sincerely to the person you have upset, move on by letting it go, and let the guilty feelings flow through the body. Whether or not the other person chooses to forgive you or hold a grudge, it is all you can do. She will need to do her own work. You do yours.

What Causes the Sacral Chakra to Close and Block Energy?

I would like to spend more time talking about blame and guilt as they are powerful emotions. The dictionary defines guilt as "the fact of having committed a specific or implied offense or crime." Emotional guilt is the feeling of having done something morally wrong. It is a reflection or judgment people put on themselves.

Guilt, as I mentioned, has a low vibrational frequency, which draws energy into the self through fear. Fear and guilt are energies of the ego. Religious guilt must be excruciatingly painful. To think God is up there somewhere in the heavens wanting us to feel guilt and shame doesn't make sense to me. We have been given a conscience that helps us choose between right and wrong, but we are not perfect. We make mistakes, we disappoint others, we hurt people, we offend, and hopefully we learn to do better. I love Maya Angelou's quote, "I did then what I knew how to do. Now that I know better, I do better."[1] In my life, sometimes it takes me a few tries to do better.

I have three values I hold myself accountable to in order to help me avoid feelings of guilt. The first is DO NO HARM. In Buddhism it is referred to as ahimsa, which means respect all things and avoid violence against others. This means with my body and my words. I wear a bracelet with the symbol of ahimsa, which looks like a hand, for a visual reminder. The second is HAVE GOOD INTENTIONS. With counseling, people come to see me because something is not working in their lives. In order to help resolve or "fix" the problem, the client must be willing to do something different. My intention is to help guide them. My motives are always pure, offering compassion and empathy, even when they leave my office not liking me and never intending to come back. The last one is to BE KIND. It is not always easy to be kind to people, particularly when they are taking out their pain and frustrations on their therapist. It is also not easy to be kind to someone who has committed a violent crime or is condescending. It can be done even though it is not easy.

---

1 "The Powerful Lesson Maya Angelou Taught Oprah," Oprah Winfrey, uploaded 10/20/11 by OWN https://www.youtube.com/watch?v=fx447ShQLeE

Blame is also fear based and comes directly from the ego. I can remember when I was younger and thought I knew it all. I would stand on my pedestal (I call it my perch) and would call my mother with my latest version of "The world according to Denise." I would say things like, "Can you believe what she said?" or "This person should know better than to act that way." My mom would listen intently and after I took a breath she would say, "You know, you're not God's assistant." I guess I needed to be knocked off my perch.

Mom was right. We need to be careful assigning blame and judgment. I had a client offer sound advice I'll never forget when he said, "Everyone can ride the bucking bronco but the guy on it." Before blaming someone else, ask yourself these questions: "Would I want to be a mayor? The governor? The president?" To be truthful, I don't even want to be the president of the HOA in our neighborhood! When I feel the need to judge other people, I tell myself to look in the mirror and start at the top!

FACT: Power and feeling the need to control people and situations are as unachievable as perfectionism. People interpret power differently. Some people feel power through money, others fame or external beauty. People who are addicted feel powerful when they are under the influence of drugs, alcohol, or other substances. These are examples of external power. True power comes from the soul.

Within your soul, where this true power lies, is your dharma. Your dharma is your purpose, the reason why God or the Universe put you on this earth and the only influence you will ever need to guide you. This is the path your soul must follow to achieve its full purpose.

Control is a myth. A person will never feel at peace until he learns to accept this fact. If he cannot, the second chakra will fluctuate between opening and closing, depending on the circumstance. Emily Maroutian wrote a powerful quote about control. She said, "Trying to control, force or manipulate anything adds more resistance"[2] which will, in turn, leave us more frustrated and out of control. The more we try to feel in control, the more out of control we feel.

How many of us spend endless hours each day trying to control situations, family, and circumstances and becoming frustrated when things are beyond our control? The one thing I have learned after years in practice is that if you want to feel more in control, you must let go of control. Sounds strange but it is the truth. Iyanla Vanzant coined a phrase I have repeated many times: "When you argue against what is, you will suffer."[3]

When we can deepen our connection with God or a higher power, we learn to trust the Divine and the Universe. This is where faith comes in. When I let go of control, my life is happier, easier, and I feel more at peace. Letting go of control has helped me develop a healthier relationship with my children. Right, kids? Feeling the need to be in control feeds the ego. The ego thinks it knows best, the ego wants to be in control, the ego can't accept what is. Let go of the ego and welcome peace. I assure you, it is worth the trade.

This is a good opportunity to talk about parenting. We believe we can control our children but, in reality, all we are doing is setting down a list of guidelines that we trust will be followed. We can lead by example, we can set limits and enforce them, but in the end

---

[2] Emily Maroutian, *The Energy of Emotions: The 10 Emotional Environments and How They Shape the World Around Us* (United States: CreateSpace Independent Publishing Platform, 2015).

[3] "Iyanla on What Happens When You Argue Against Reality," Iyanla Vanzant, uploaded 7/30/12 by OWN https://www.youtube.com/watch?v=59HtLZ2ryz8

we are trusting our children to carry out the values we have instilled in them. But we are not in control, and we need to understand the difference between leading by example and forcefully manipulating for the sake of having power over someone else.

Sex can be healthy and beautiful. It can also be traumatic and painful. When we are in a healthy sexual relationship with someone we trust and are connected to, our second chakra will have good energy flow. When we have been violated sexually, it will close.

Money is energy: I have learned it is a waste of energy to worry about money. My husband and I have been in private practice for many years. When I started focusing on money in the past, our practices started to slow down and money didn't come in. The more I worried, the worse things got. I started to put my trust in my dharma. If we were meant to stay in private practice, the patients and the money would follow. I had to trust God to provide. All we needed to do was to provide the three A's: Affability, Ability, and Accountability.

Creativity is an energy flow that can be used to expand our imagination, solve problems, and create beauty in the world. It can also be used to manipulate, deceive, and cause harm. Using our creative minds for personal gain and hurting others will block the second chakra and manifest physically over time.

The Physical or Psychological Effect of Blocked Energy at the Second Chakra

When our second chakra is blocked for a long period of time, the body will begin to manifest symptoms. I have learned how to check energy in the body. Energy actually emits from the body. Holding a pendulum in front of the chakras will cause it to move on its own if energy is flowing over the chakra. If the energy is blocked, the pendulum will stay perfectly still. I find this tool extremely helpful to confirm intuitions when I am working with patients.

It is not unusual for a female patient to come to counseling after she has discovered her husband has been unfaithful. It is also likely she may be experiencing **irregular periods, pelvic pain, no menstrual cycle,** or **back pain** since learning of her husband's infidelity. This is because her second chakra has blocked, a result of feelings such as guilt, blame, and unhealthy relationships with money and sex. The physical changes in her body add to the emotional pain. I have seen even the healthiest women manifest physically when the second chakra has blocked.

Infertility can also be an issue when the second chakra is blocked and vice versa. If you are a woman, think about how difficult it is to conceive when month after month you are not pregnant after desperately trying to have a baby. The guilt can be overwhelming.

In men, particularly young men, the second chakra is usually open. Their sex drive is high and they have a tendency to have a lot of energy flow in this area. Financial struggles for men can cause decreased libido when this chakra becomes blocked.

My Story

In 2007, we left our home in Baltimore to move to Florida so my husband could open a private practice. Four years before, we had designed and built a very large home in northwest Baltimore, which was to be sold. Feeling sure our house in Baltimore would sell quickly, we bought a house in Florida and made plans to put an addition on in order to accommodate our family of five.

As many of you remember, perhaps painfully, this was the beginning of the housing bubble burst. We found ourselves stuck with two homes and a costly addition while the money flew out of our bank account as if it had powerful wings.

I can't remember ever feeling so stressed in my life. I manage all the bills, and I kept a lot of the reality of our drowning debt from my husband. He was working over twelve hours a day and didn't need me adding to his already heavy load.

At this time, I went in for my yearly gynecological appointment for a routine check. I have always been very healthy and had no reason to think that day would be any exception. The doctor examined me and said, "You are going to need to have this fibroid removed from your uterus because it is massive." I looked at him and said, "What fibroid?"

Six weeks later, I had a total hysterectomy. I played tennis and worked out at the gym the day before. I had no idea why this had happened until years later when it all connected. We had financial struggles, I felt guilty for convincing my husband that moving to Florida was the right move, I blamed my husband and myself for not accepting the first low offer we'd received on our home in Baltimore a week after we put it on the market. My second chakra was blocked for years while we were recovering financially, and my body had paid the price.

Case Study

I had a thirty-year-old married woman come to my office a few years ago wanting help for anxiety. She and her husband had been trying for years to get pregnant, and it was all she could think about. They had tried IVF and were struggling financially after paying for it. Although she wanted to try IVF again, it was a gamble, since it hadn't worked the first time.

This client had a strange relationship with her mother, who controlled her through manipulation and guilt. She never felt good enough, and her mother made it her business to know all her business. My client's anxiety was palpable. She routinely spent the entire hour we were together defending everything she had been doing in her life, hoping she had lived up to her mother's expectations.

As you can see, many factors contributed to the client's psychological struggles as well as the impact it had on her physically. She came to me for about six months but had trouble breaking free from the toxic and inappropriate relationship with her mother. She came back one time, after I hadn't seen her in over a year. She still had not become pregnant.

How to Open the Sacral Chakra

Take responsibility for yourself and resist the urge to blame others, regardless if you are right or not.

Let go of guilt by creating a set of personal values you will honor for yourself.

Remember this quote: "No matter what you do, someone will always talk about you. Someone will always question your judgment. Someone will always doubt you. So just smile and make the choices you can live with."

Set boundaries.

Don't get caught up looking for power externally through money, fame, vanity, addiction.

Honor your word, your ethics, your morals, and your higher power.

Practice ahimsa, which comes from Buddhism and means "respect for all living things and avoidance of violence toward others."

Give yourself the gift of therapy.

Find someone to help you heal.

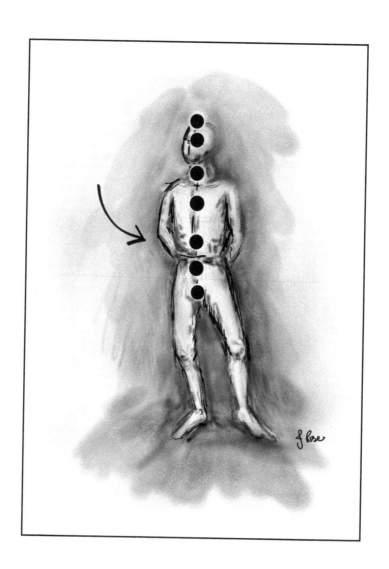

Chapter 4

The Third Chakra: The Solar Plexus Chakra— The Energy behind the Relationship with Ourselves

Understanding this Energy

This energy is located at the solar plexus, which is more easily described as the abdomen or the stomach. It includes our intestines, liver, kidneys, gallbladder, and the middle portion of our back, which is directly behind the abdomen.

If you don't learn anything else by reading this book, pay attention to this chapter. Do you ever wonder why people are so overweight? Why do so many turn to alcohol to cope with life? Why are we so sensitive to what others think? Why do we feel the need to win? Why do we ruminate (overthink) about the silliest of decisions? Well, thank the third chakra for it.

What Causes the Solar Plexus Chakra to Close and Block Energy?

This is the energy of the inner self, the relationship we have with ourselves. This chakra is connected to our feelings of self-worth. Earlier I mentioned feeling a knot in my stomach when someone betrayed my trust. Trust is a feeling we allow when we let our guard down and are vulnerable. We trust someone to not hurt us, to protect us, to love us. When that trust is betrayed, we feel it in our stomach. Sometimes, we get a bad feeling someone isn't trustworthy even though that person is nice to us. Thank the third chakra again!

Being overly sensitive to criticism will cause the third chakra to block. When someone hurts our feelings, we feel shame, inadequacy, and inferiority. Then, where do we go for ease? Right to the refrigerator!

Have you ever thought about why people overeat? Because they are always hungry? Obesity runs in their family? They were diagnosed with a physiological condition that causes weight gain? The explanations are endless. People will try every diet known to man regardless of the statistics showing 95% of people who go on a diet will gain the weight back. Think about that statistic for a minute. If I asked you to invest in a stock and told you that you had a 95% chance of losing money, do you think you would consider investing in it? Probably not. Yet, people are desperate to lose weight. They are so desperate, they will endure gastric bypass, gastric sleeves, or gastric bands or eat cabbage soup, no carbs, no sugar, you name it.

I enjoy public speaking. Years ago, I gave a talk called "It's not what you're eating but what's eating you." When the third chakra blocks, the body will overeat to fulfill a need. The need is to feel relief from the emotional and mental struggles they have not yet dealt with. The hurt can be so deep, it causes some to ruminate. The word ruminate comes from the word ruminant, which is an animal that chews its cud. To ruminate means going over and over something in your mind. You overthink.

Overthinking is a waste of time and is another thing people do that causes the third chakra to block. Make a decision and let it go! My dad used to say, "There is no such thing as a poor decision. At the very least, you can serve as a horrible example." Think about it this way. When we make a decision, we make the best possible choice we are able to at that time with the knowledge and experience we have. If it is a poor choice, it will serve as a lesson for us to grow.

I occasionally spend time with an overthinker, maybe in session or in my personal life. A conversation with an overthinker sounds something like this:

"My son's coach called to ask me to make brownies for the team this week but I said no. It isn't that I didn't want to make the brownies, but I had to take my mother-in-law to the doctor for tests. Plus, my father had a heart attack last week, and I promised my mother I would pick up his prescriptions from the pharmacy. I probably could have made the brownies but I didn't have any flour. I don't know why I didn't have any flour, but I couldn't check the pantry because I had to work overtime because one of the secretaries had to leave early because she was sick. You know, I have made brownies for the team several times. In fact, I am usually in charge of the list. I just can't keep up with all of this. Maybe I'll go to the grocery store and buy brownies. This way it will be over and done with, and no one will need to worry about it."

The entire time I'm listening to this person, I'm in my mind quoting the line from *My Big Fat Greek Wedding*, "Please let this be the end of this conversation." But unfortunately, they are just getting warmed up. By the time they finally finish, I am EXHAUSTED. I may have tried to interrupt the thought pattern by adding a sentence like, "You don't have to convince me," but to no avail. In session, I might say, "Why are you explaining all of this to me?" but nothing I say appears to work. This line of thinking leads to self-sabotage, resulting from the need to please. Pleasers are vulnerable to manipulators because they can't say no.

Low self-esteem: A person with self-confidence and one who is grounded (first chakra) has clearly defined boundaries. Boundaries are what separates us from others. It is important for others to know what your boundaries are, what you are willing to do or tolerate, and what you are not willing to do or tolerate.

A person with poor boundaries is subject to the thoughts and opinions of others. If everyone had to rely on the opinions of others, it would be impossible to get anything accomplished. We would be paralyzed with fear, and we would never take a risk.

Fear is a powerful emotion and is caused by blockage in the flow of energy. Fear is uncomfortable but it is not harmful. Our mind would disagree. The mind works overtime because it is petrified of feeling fear. Almost everything I can think of that keeps people from feeling peace is fear based. Many religions are fear based. How about politics? The world will come to an end if you are a Republican or a Democrat? And the news? Fear, fear, fear will keep you tuning in so ratings increase, and we can create more worry, more stress, and more fear.

No wonder we are overeating and out of balance. Peace does not occur when everything around us is well. Peace is when the world is as it is and we feel peace within ourselves. I wish you all peace.

Lacking self-respect will block the third chakra and often lead to drinking. I have worked with many clients struggling with alcohol who have all said a similar thing, "I drink because I have no respect for myself." It must be incredibly painful to feel little or no sense of self-worth. The energy behind this feeling is a low-vibrational energy that is not only low, it is also very slow. It is not uncommon for someone who has been binge drinking for days to stop eating and bathing.

Before working in a rehabilitation facility specializing in addiction, I was required to attend a dozen or more AA meetings. Fortunately, AA meetings are offered in every county and in every state. I had several meetings to choose from, and I attended many in my hometown. I loved going. I took a notebook, took pages of notes, and learned as much as I ever did in graduate school. I found the speakers to be honest, raw, and genuine. The common denominator with every story was an overwhelming feeling of low **self-worth**, where they turned to the only thing that gave them relief…alcohol. Some in recovery lost their marriages, others lost jobs or money. One lady killed two people while driving drunk. All of these people, regular people like you and me, had turned to alcohol for ease.

The Physical or Psychological Effect of Blocked Energy at the Third Chakra

In the third chakra, where low self-esteem lies and alcohol soothes, **liver problems** develop. **Diabetes** is a disease manifested by energy blocking in the third chakra, which can lead to overeating and lack of exercise. **Hepatitis** and **arthritis** are also linked to a blockage of energy at the third chakra.

Blocking at the third chakra is where eating disorders originate. Eating disorders are very serious. I was a critical care nurse and have been a nurse for nearly thirty years. Critical care nurses are known to be quick on their feet, fearless, and not easily intimidated. We have to be. There are times when decisions need to be made on a dime and physicians rely on the ICU nurse to pick up and relay vital information to them. That being said, an anorexic patient scares me more than any critical care patient ever did. Typically, people who suffer from anorexia are women in their twenties, convinced they will feel better about themselves and their problems will go away when they get their weight down to say 100 pounds. They starve, they exercise, they take laxatives, they are deceptive, they are ruthless. When they reach the 100-pound mark, they don't feel any better psychologically than they did 5 or 10 pounds ago, so they commit to losing more weight. This becomes dangerous to their health, particularly for the heart because their electrolytes, potassium, and magnesium are depleted. Some people with eating disorders starve, others binge and purge, many just binge, desperately trying to find ease, to feel better about themselves, looking for something to feel right while ultimately looking to open the third chakra.

My Story

Birthdays can be hard for some people. My fortieth birthday was tough for me. I remember talking about my fortieth birthday for months before the big day on July 1st. It was "all about me," and I was turning forty with all smiles until it came to the day when I realized I had turned forty. For a week I was depressed and couldn't figure out why. All of a sudden, I figured it out. At forty, my life was probably half over and there were still so many things I hadn't accomplished. The big one was my weight. I had been married for about three years and had gained fifteen pounds. Every week I said, "I need to lose weight" or "Next week I'm going to get serious," but weeks turned into months and months turned into years of being fifteen pounds overweight.

I decided to get serious about losing weight and hired a personal trainer. His name was Charles, and he looked like a black Mr. Clean. He was tough, he expected me to work hard, and I was up for the challenge. It didn't take me long to be in the best shape of my life. Unfortunately, I was still 15 pounds overweight. I told Charles I was happy with my workouts, but I wasn't sure why I still couldn't lose weight. He said, "It is not what you do in the gym, it is what you do when you walk out of the gym."

I realized it was up to me to do the work. I was going to change my eating habits. The problem was, I later realized, eating eased my late-night anxiety. I would eat after the kids went to bed to reward myself for making it through a busy day, taking care of the house and my husband, working, and raising three kids. Food was my "lovey," and I had to get to the root of my eating before my weight would budge.

For me, the relationship I had with myself was unhealthy. I didn't feel as if some people in my life respected me. I made decisions based on fear. I was sensitive to criticism, and I needed to go back to counseling and work through a few things. I'm so glad I did.

Case Study

When a person decides to have gastric bypass, gastric sleeve surgery, or lap band surgery, a psychological clearance is mandatory.

The reason for the evaluation is to rule out a psychological factor contributing to the patient's morbid obesity. These patients typically have the same complaints when they arrive at their surgeon's office. They have failed to lose weight despite having tried diet after diet and feel they have no other option than to have surgery. It is interesting to hear many of them say, "This will be the tool I need to help me get to a healthy weight."

I complete the psychological evaluation and fax their clearance over to the surgeon. If I don't, they will find someone who will. I know overeating fulfills a need. The energy is blocked in the third chakra. I have rarely seen the patient back in my office after their initial visit but occasionally do, sometimes years later. I have never known surgery to cure the problem, although I am certain some people would beg to differ with me. Unfortunately, if the underlying problem is not corrected, the patient may eat his way back to obesity despite a perfectly performed surgery.

How to Open the Solar Plexus Chakra

When we **practice self-love and self-care**, we benefit not only ourselves but everyone around us. If we are happy, our partner is more likely to be happy, our children will be happy, people whom we work with will be happy.

Meditation: I had a client lose 30 pounds by meditating. She said she realized she was an emotional eater and meditated every evening. She said her desire to overeat disappeared.

Create a vision board: Remember that energy flows where it is directed. A vision board can help you clarify your goals and intentions.

Counseling: I am not recommending you see a counselor because I am one. I know counseling works. It can be essential to have an objective person help you explore deep-seated feelings of low self-worth, fear, lack of trust, and so on.

Hypnosis: Hypnosis can help clear inaccurate thoughts and feelings. We mentioned the benefits of hypnosis earlier.

Reiki/Energy work: You can find someone who practices energy work in every state. I highly recommend you give it a try. A person certified in this type of practice can help open the chakras.

Acupuncture: Acupuncture is helpful for pain and effective release of chi.

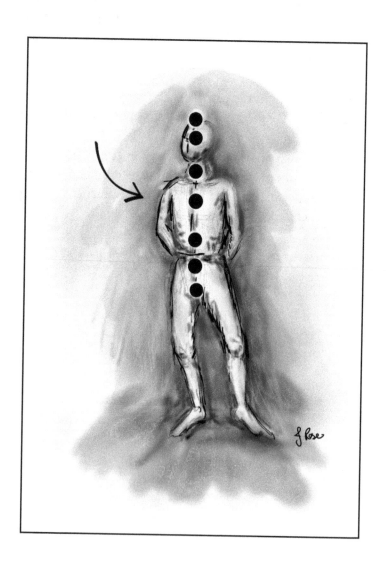

Chapter 5

The Fourth Chakra
The Heart Chakra—
The Powerhouse of Our Soul

Understanding this Energy

This energy sits behind the **heart** and **lungs**. It also includes bones around the heart like the **ribs, shoulders**, and **arms**. Over the heart are our **breasts** and below the heart is the **diaphragm**.

What Causes the Heart Chakra to Close and Block Energy?

Think about some of the emotions that come from the heart. The most obvious are love, hope, trust, compassion, and forgiveness. These are high-vibrational energies, and we can feel someone's heart when they are sincere and thoughtful. These energies don't block the heart chakra, they open it and allow energy to flow. We can feel someone's heart when his heart is open, and we can also sense it when someone doesn't love us, regardless of what he says.

Negative emotions can cause the heart chakra to block: feelings like **bitterness** and **resentment**. **Grief** and **loneliness** can not only close the heart chakra, they can cause serious heart problems. When someone is overwhelmed by grief, perhaps when a spouse passes away after fifty years of marriage, it is not surprising when he follows shortly thereafter. We would describe the partner as having died from a broken heart.

Have you ever met someone you couldn't get a vibe from? You may have described her as cold, selfish, self-absorbed, disconnected. Regardless of how you described the feeling, what you may have been trying to say is you couldn't feel his heart. I try to be mindful of my heart chakra when I practice. In fact, I include it when I spend time grounding in the morning. When you are a counselor, you treat many of the same issues hundreds of times. You have seen it, heard it, and can often predict where the story is going before the patient finishes telling it. Even though I have "been there and done that," I never want to lose sight of the fact that this is their story, their struggle, their heartache, their journey. Opening my heart chakra, returning phone calls, checking in, being on time, and truly caring about all my clients allows my clients to feel my heart. I pray for compassion, I pray for empathy, I pray for guidance from God, I pray for wisdom.

Out of all the conditions I treat, **anxiety** is by far the most common. Chronic anxiety will affect the heart because the condition causes the heart chakra to close. There were times when I'd be driving in my car, not in a hurry, nothing major on my mind, and it would hit me. I'd start to feel a slight tightness in my chest. Even though I was convinced my heart was just fine, I went to see a hypnotherapist. She told me that even though I was not aware of why my chest was tightening, which I described as feeling like a glop of black sludge sitting on my chest, she said my body knew. After she hypnotized me, she helped me learn tools including visualization and a technique called the emotional freedom technique (EFT) that I still practice. This has helped me reduce anxiety and have fewer episodes of chest discomfort.

Anxiety is fake fear. It is our perception something is dangerous even when it is not harmful. Again, the body doesn't know the difference between what is real and what is imagined, and the effects are the same. This is why anxiety can cause someone to go to the emergency room thinking he was having a heart attack when the heart is physically normal. Other symptoms of anxiety include flushing of the skin, increased heart rate (tachycardia), dry mouth, sweating (diaphoresis), muscle tension, rapid breathing (tachypnea), dizziness or fainting (syncope), and headaches.

To screen for anxiety and to determine the severity of a patient's symptoms, I take out a pile of colored index cards. Each card provides a description of what psychologists call a cognitive distortion. A cognitive distortion is a fancy term for "stinking thinking." They are thoughts or perceptions we think are rational but actually are irrational.

How many of the following examples of stinking thinking are you able to connect to?

1. Emotional reasoning: Feelings must be true. I feel stupid and, therefore, I am stupid.

2. Jumping to conclusions: Mind reading or fortune telling. "I know what she is thinking..."

3. Heaven's reward fallacy: We feel bitter because we haven't been rewarded or recognized.

4. Control fallacies: We feel helpless and a victim.

73

5. Fallacy of change: We need to change someone else because our hopes for happiness seem to depend entirely on him. "I need the boy at school to like me so I can be happy."

6. Fallacy of fairness: Life should be fair.

7. Shoulds: A list of strict rules about how we or others should behave. I like to call this one "shoulda, coulda, woulda," and the consequence for this type of irrational thinking is guilt.

8. Overgeneralization: When we come to a general conclusion based on a single incident. "If it happened once, it will likely happen again." This type of irrational thinking is where panic stems from.

9. Personalization: Believing everything others do or say is some kind of reaction to us personally. "I know that email the boss sent out was directed at me."

10. Catastrophizing: We expect a disaster no matter what: making a mountain out of the proverbial molehill.

11. Polarized or black-and-white thinking: Either/or with no middle ground. This type of irrational thinking is based on power and position rather than on principle: "My way or the highway."

12. Always being right: Feeling the need to win instead of being heard.

13. Filtering: When we take the negative details and magnify them while filtering out all the positive aspects of the situation. We may think this helps us prepare for the worst possible scenario, but it actually causes the

body to suffer by anticipating an event that may or may not happen.

14. Global labeling: We generalize one or two qualities into a negative global judgment. This type of irrational thinking is how stereotypes and prejudices develop.

15. Blaming: When we hold other people responsible for our pain. "You are the reason I am miserable." The reality is no one makes us do or feel anything. We choose to react the way we do. We need to learn to take responsibility for our emotions and perceive them in a non-harmful way.[1]

Lack of forgiveness: When it is a question of who is right and who is wrong, and we refuse to forgive, our heart chakra closes. When we become self-absorbed with anxiety and anger, we push people away and the chakra blocks. When we trust no one, we are unable to get close to each other and enjoy the richness of relationships. When we go through life waiting for something or someone to betray us, we often get what we fear the most. This is what happens when we focus our energy on a particular thought or direction, regardless of whether we want something to happen or not.

The Physical or Psychological Effect of Blocked Energy at the Fourth Chakra

Physiologically, **heart and lung** problems develop from a blocked heart chakra. Many people smoke to relieve the discomfort

---

[1] "15 Common Cognitive Distortions," Psych Central, accessed September 14, 2020, https://psychcentral.com/lib/15-common- cognitive-distortions/

of this blockage, which we talked about already. They say, "Smoking relieves my stress," which feels true because the deep inhalation and exhalation from smoking will open the heart chakra. The problem is the ease created from smoking is not healthy.

Heart problems include heart attacks, heart failure, and an enlarged heart. I would say the younger ICU patients who were admitted after having a heart attack were typically type A personalities who were overworked, stressed out, overweight, and who were living life on the edge of a mental breakdown. Confining them to a bed connected to a cardiac monitor was pure torture for them, I remember.

Lung problems include allergies, asthma, and pneumonia. When the heart chakra is blocked, energy is unable to flow around the lungs and our breathing is affected. Stress will cause our breathing to become very shallow.

I have had the privilege of seeing clients who were referred to me to help them cope with cancer, many going through chemotherapy and/or radiation for treatment. It took a lot of work on my own to prepare me for it. It was heartbreaking to see people, once vibrant and thriving, now balding, weak, haggard, and dying. I'd had plenty of experience working with sick and dying patients in the ICU, but this was different. These patients were actively fighting for their lives, suffering, scared, and sick.

Many cancer referrals were women battling breast cancer. I typically asked them to tell me what their life was like before they were diagnosed. Their stories were very much the same: a moderate to severe degree of anxiety, bitterness, resentment, loneliness, or grief. I was amazed by the connection. I mustered up the courage to call one of the oncologists who referred to me the most. He was a neighbor, a mentor, Hindu, and, most of all, compassionate and caring. Touching as lightly as I could on the subject, I asked him if he believed in energy blocking and whether or not he thought it contributed to cancer. He said, "Absolutely, but don't forget to add stress and sugar to the equation because cancer loves those two things also."

Again, it added up. It was clear: dis-ease comes from the blocking of energy. It could be in the stomach, in the throat, in the pelvis, wherever it can find a place to host. My job as a clinician was clear: heal the mind and nurture the spirit, and the body will stay healthy. The only challenge was convincing my patients I was onto something.

My Story

I have endless energy it seems. Our grandmother was the same way and many family members call me "Miss Dollie" because I remind them of her. I always seem to find that extra gear when I need it, which is why the sickest ICU patient rarely overwhelmed me. I used to drive a blue car and my neighbor called me "the blue flash" because I was always out and about doing things. When I visited my mother, she used to call me "the little fairy" because I flitted around her house cleaning and organizing everything in sight. My husband calls me "the white tornado," which I'm sure he means in an endearing way regardless of how it sounds.

If anyone who knows me well walked into my house and noticed clothes all over the place, the bed unmade, and mail all over the counter, she would run to the phone and call 911.

I love being neat, tidy, and organized. It is one of the things I am grateful for, because it allows me to do a lot of work without feeling frazzled. However, I had to learn balance.

When I was in my late twenties, I saw a therapist because I was stressed out! I talked to the therapist about all the balls I had up in the air: new baby, 60 pound weight loss, going to school, and working full time. When I finally came up for air, he said, "If you keep it up, you will slowly kill yourself."

I realized I needed balance after seeing that therapist but it took years to figure it out. Trying to convince clients how important it is for the body to incorporate balance between doing and being is the most challenging part of what I do in therapy. I sometimes think I could convince someone to commit a crime faster than I could convince him to take the time to enjoy his life. How sad is that?

Case Study

I had a very attractive woman come into my office who was in her mid-forties. As I walked her back to my office, her anxiety was palpable. She answered my questions with "I'm worried because," "I feel guilty about," "I'm afraid of," or "I'm nervous because."

Anxiety is a paradox, I discovered. People who are anxious have a tendency to worry about the little things but aren't as concerned about the things they should be. This particular client worried when her children didn't get good grades. She feared other parents might be thinking she wasn't a good enough mother. She felt guilty when she couldn't please someone. The list was endless.

This client had married a narcissist. He was in the sales business and spent a lot of time out of town. He was mean to her, put hands on her occasionally, and he had a wandering eye. He brought home and shared a sexually transmitted disease with her, but she still couldn't leave him. Instead, she blamed him for ruining her life. She screamed at him, and their arguments became physical.

She had the education and the ability to move out and be on her own, but she chose to stay paralyzed with fear because she wasn't sure how a divorce would affect the children.

I saw this client for many months. She cancelled several appointments because she had bronchitis (heart chakra). She gained 25 pounds (stomach chakra), and her periods became irregular (pelvic chakra). It was sad to see.

When I felt the time was right, I had a heart-to-heart talk with her. I told her she had two choices: either she could stay in the marriage, knowing things would not likely get better and her husband would not likely change—or—she could look for a job and move forward in her life on her own. I reassured her I would support her with whatever she decided to do, but a decision needed to be made.

I received an email from this client weeks later. It was several pages long, and she said she felt very betrayed by me for not supporting her and taking her side. I was her third therapist. I called her and told her I was sorry she felt I had betrayed her and asked her to come in so we could talk about it. She never did. Her husband called me later and said she would not be back.

How to Open the Heart Chakra

Opening the heart chakra takes courage. We close the heart chakra in an attempt to protect ourselves from pain and suffering. Unfortunately, we end up attracting more pain and suffering.

Negative feelings and emotions, fear-based feelings, cause us to suck energy in like a vacuum, as I mentioned earlier. Fear-based emotions focus on the self. Positive reframing of feelings and emotions, which are based on love and compassion, will shift our focus and energy away or out of the body. Examples include things like offering to help someone in need, offering compassion, being kind, listening, volunteering, humanitarianism.

If you are grieving, make an appointment with a counselor or join a support group. If you are resentful and bitter, have the courage to forgive. Forgiveness allows you to move forward, and it is something you do for yourself.

Trust your gut when you don't feel someone's heart and resist the urge to please. It is better to walk away from an abusive relationship and model strength for your children. Remember, your children are watching and learning from you.

Define the feeling underneath the anger and speak it. Yelling won't make someone hear you. If anything, it will do the opposite.

Work with a therapist, love yourself first, set clear boundaries, and teach others how to treat you.

Do the work and your heart chakra will open. When it does, the love will flow from your soul. People will feel it, and they will be blessed by it.

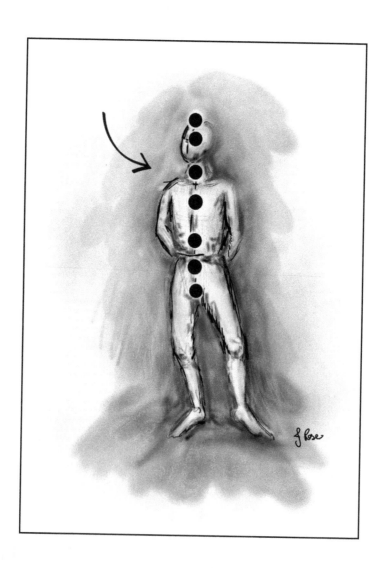

Chapter 6

The Fifth Chakra: The Throat Chakra— The Energy behind Speaking Our Truth

Understanding this Energy

Visualize this energy, which is located behind the throat, for a moment. This energy includes the mouth (teeth, gums, jaw), neck and thyroid, trachea, and the esophagus. It is located above the heart but below the third eye, which is in between the eyebrows.

What Causes the Throat Chakra to Close and Block Energy?

This is the energy behind our ability to **express ourselves**. Have you ever noticed a speaker stand up in front of their audience, begin to speak, and then clear his throat because his voice was not audibly clear? Many speakers have a glass of water nearby to help clear the throat chakra. Once the speaker gets going, his hoarseness appears to resolve on its own as the throat chakra opens and his anxiety lessens. If the chakra stays closed, the speaker may stutter or be unable to articulate his thoughts the way he envisioned. How embarrassing this must feel! Public speaking can be challenging for this reason alone.

Imagine how it must feel to have no one care to hear what you have to say? It is not uncommon for teens or young adults to question their sexuality. However, many cultures, not to mention society in general, do not accept homosexuality, transgenderism, or gender-fluid sexual preferences. It must be excruciatingly painful to feel alone and afraid just because your sexual desires are not within the societal norm. I can feel this kind of pain in my throat. A teenager who doesn't feel herself heard or who never learned to communicate appropriately and effectively will sometimes start drinking or experimenting with drugs to find relief.

Sensitivity to judgment and criticism: You would be amazed at how many clients I have seen who care deeply about what other people think about them. They worry what complete strangers think of them. They mind read, fortune tell, all because they want to be liked and accepted. These feelings will cause the energy to block around the throat, which will prevent us from setting limits and boundaries.

Not having the freedom to follow your dharma: We have all been placed on this earth with different likes, different gifts, different abilities, and sometimes differences in our sexual interests.

Our dharma is our path, our purpose, the way we feel comfortable going through life based on our dreams, our hopes, our desires, and our abilities. Can you imagine how painful it must be when you are unable to follow your dharma because of religion, race, sex, identity, or our culture? When we are not allowed to express ourselves authentically, the chakra behind the throat will close.

Our throat chakra will block energy when we **lack confidence in making decisions**. These people agonize over choices, require a lot of reassurance, ask multiple people for advice, second-guess themselves, overthink, and care too much about the opinions of others. You get the picture.

The Physical or Psychological Effect of Blocked Energy at the Fifth Chakra

Symptoms include **mouth ulcers, TMJ disorder, thyroid problems, raspy throat,** and **chronic laryngitis**. The most common I see by far is thyroid problems.

My Story

For years, I would feel as if I couldn't swallow when I was stressed. I would tell myself, "There is nothing wrong with you, just swallow," but I felt like I was trying to swallow the pit of a peach. When I felt like people weren't listening to me, especially my immediate family, I couldn't swallow. It was both frustrating and uncomfortable.

I was born in New Jersey and things you have probably heard about Jersey girls are true. We have a reputation for speaking our minds, and I had an edge about me. Unfortunately, my opinions were not always heard, which left me annoyed and irritable. I, like my dad, would resort to sarcasm. I thought I was funny. Dr. Timothy Tehan, who is still my therapist, said I was emasculating and "too classy to stoop to that level." I remember leaving his office shocked. He was also the counselor who told me I was passive-aggressive. Although I didn't like hearing it, I trusted him. Dr. Tehan is a New Yorker (got to love them); he shoots from the hip just as I did. I knew he was right, and I knew I had to change.

My husband was instrumental in helping me speak up and lose the edge. I credit him to this day for smoothing out many of my rough edges, even though there were many times I didn't want to listen to what he had to say. Over the years, my husband, Harvey, has made me a better person. I have learned to use my voice, speak my truth, articulate clearly, and spell correctly, and I've tried my hardest not to change tenses while writing a letter. Everyone should have someone strong enough to handle a Jersey girl in her corner.

Case Study

I had a client who came into his first session wearing a top hat. He was in his thirties, gay, a cross-dresser, and had a condition known in psychology as paraphilic infantilism. He wore a diaper, kept a pacifier in his pocket, and slept in a crib made for an adult. Believe it or not, there is a company somewhere that sells supplies and equipment to adults with this condition. I was just an intern when I met him, but he was a client I would never forget. He had a raspy throat and cleared his throat throughout our sessions together. He was lonely and felt misunderstood. He was a burly guy, looked like a football player, but he was also gay and loved to wear a skirt. His parents tried to understand him but had a hard time embracing his lifestyle. He was dependent on his parents to support him financially, as he was unable to hold down a job. He was lost, he was vulnerable, he was afraid. I remember him burping in session. He would say, "Excuse me," and burp loudly. He would tell story after story about his friends and how they took advantage of him. I felt his pain in my throat as well as my heart.

How to Open the Throat Chakra

There are many ways to open each chakra. Many of the methods, tools, and recommendations I have offered may be similar. I have tried to keep the list fairly short, and you may be able to add a few more. Here are just a few tips to help open the throat chakra.

Aromatherapy: I use aromatherapy in my home and in the office where I work. I diffuse essential oils, choosing different oils to enhance emotions. I have a guide I use in the shape of a wheel. If I'm looking to enhance an emotion (peace, comfort, fear, anger, sadness), I look up the recommended oil and diffuse it. Some of the recommended oils to help open the heart chakra are jasmine, sage, clove, lavender, and peppermint.

Positive affirmations: When you speak highly of yourself, the throat chakra will begin to open. What you have to say matters. God has given you a voice. Speak your truth.

Guided meditation: I love to meditate. Guided meditations are my favorite because they help me to have someone remind me to breathe and be still. The breath is full, deep, and intentional. The practice helps me get into my parasympathetic nervous system. When I do, it is peaceful, it is safe, and it opens the throat chakra as well as all the energies in my body.

Singing a mantra: I met with a woman for business, and she began asking me questions about my job. Somewhere in the conversation, I mentioned practicing yoga. She quickly stopped me and told me she was a Christian, and she would never practice yoga because they chant in yoga, and she believed it was sacrilegious to chant. I continued talking about energy, the various illnesses caused by blocked energy, and the importance of having tools to help open our energy gates, the chakras. I asked her if she had ever thought about why people sing in church. She said it was a way to connect to God. She was right. When we sing, the vibrations of the music help us open our chakras, allowing us to commune with God. In yoga, chanting "OMM" acknowledges our connection to everything in the world and in the Universe. I told her I wasn't sure what part of that displeased God. She said she didn't know either.

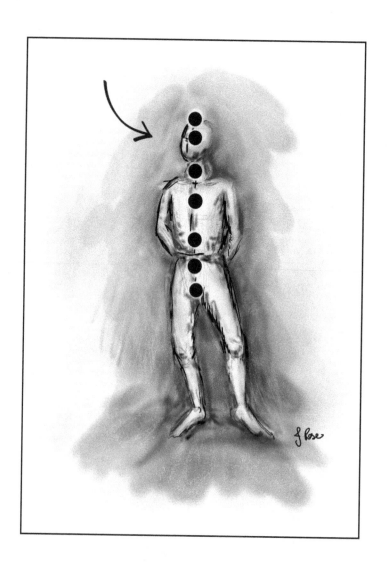

Chapter 7

The Sixth Chakra: The Third Eye Chakra— An Intellectual Being

Understanding this Energy

This energy is located between the eyes and involves the **brain, our eyes, ears**, and **nose**. It is also connected to our pituitary gland. This gland has been called the "master gland" because it causes certain organs to secrete hormones, depending on what the body needs. The pineal gland is also in this energetic field. This gland regulates melatonin, which helps with sleep.

When we are open-minded, we learn lessons and gain wisdom. We are more willing to push through fear—fears within ourselves, and fears which result from narrow-minded thinking. We are more logical and less emotional with problems and in situations. The Buddhist practice of detachment can be applied to the energies within the sixth chakra, which is also known as the third eye.

When I talk about detachment in session, some clients resist because they think that detaching means not caring, acting cold or callous. Yet it is possible to feel compassion and concern without attaching emotionally. With nursing and psychology, it is a necessity to avoid burnout.

What Causes the Third Eye Chakra to Close and Block Energy?

I have seen the third eye blocked with an **intellectual or developmental delay**. I have picked up many of these in children by checking the energy around the third eye. Checking energy is an assessment tool I use but do not rely on solely to make a diagnosis. I will also refer the child for psychological testing and evaluation performed by a licensed psychologist.

Other factors that will block the third eye are feelings of inadequacy, a lack of empathy, and a closed-minded outlook. I will offer an interesting case study later in this chapter.

The Physical or Psychological Effect of Blocked Energy at the Sixth Chakra

Physical manifestations or illnesses resulting from blockage in this chakra include **learning problems, stroke, brain hemorrhage, neurological problems**, and **seizures**.

My Story

I wish someone had checked my energy when I was a child. I'd be willing to bet my sixth chakra was blocked. I had a difficult time retaining information in school, and I was a terrible test taker. I have never been formally diagnosed, but I am fairly sure I have a processing disorder and maybe even mild dyslexia. My dad said I wasn't very smart and, based on my grades, he was accurate.

I worked with a tutor in middle school who helped me discover I learn best visually. I started writing down facts and information on index cards, which improved my grades significantly. I made stacks of index cards when I took my nursing boards, my comps, my national psychology boards, and even the Florida state boards. I still use index cards to evaluate anxiety and depression. When I don't use index cards, I draw the concept on a piece of paper.

My sixth chakra has excellent energy flow. I continue to study. I am open to exploring new ideas, methods, and treatments in my field. I know traditional talk therapy isn't the only answer. I just needed to be willing to get uncomfortable and try something new.

Case Study

I was seeing a young man around the age of twelve or thirteen. His mother said he had been bullied at school and had anger issues. As I got to know this delightful young man, I learned the bullying and the anger were only part of his struggle. His father was emotionally abusive, not only to him but also to his mother. I recommended Mom come in with Dad separately to meet with me.

When Mom and Dad came in together, I could feel Dad's negative energy as he sat down. Although he was somewhat polite, I could feel his anger, and I could only imagine what he was like when he wasn't on his best behavior. We began talking about the couple's son, his anger, the bullying at school, when I apparently struck a nerve with Dad. He looked up at my diplomas on the wall and said, "Since you are so smart with all your diplomas on the wall, why don't you tell us what is going on?" I quickly offered some firm, but kind, limit setting, which Mom later told me she had never seen anyone do. This was precisely the problem.

My patient's mom was a pleaser, his dad an erupter and a narcissist. The family came back for another session, and my client told his dad he wanted me to check his dad's energy. Believe it or not, Dad agreed. As predicted, he was blocked at grounding, blocked at the abdomen (sensitivity to criticism and trust), blocked at the sixth chakra (feelings of adequacy and spirituality). He was living his life based on ego; perhaps he had many unresolved issues. Unfortunately, his legacy of hurt and pain was being passed onto his son. Cases like this are the ones therapists never forget.

How to Open the Third Eye Chakra

Understand and honor your beliefs and values but be open to and respect the beliefs and values of others without hate, criticism, or judgment.

When you are bothered or annoyed by something someone says or does, look within yourself to gain a better understanding of your own weaknesses and insecurities.

Look at mistakes, poor decisions, and poor choices as opportunities to grow.

Never speak negatively about yourself.

Practice detachment. Feel compassion and voice concern without feeling the need to rescue or take on responsibilities that are not yours.

Pray to God for wisdom and understand there is a higher purpose for what you are going through, regardless of whether it makes sense to you or not.

Trust: trust God, trust yourself, trust the energies within you, trust your intuition.

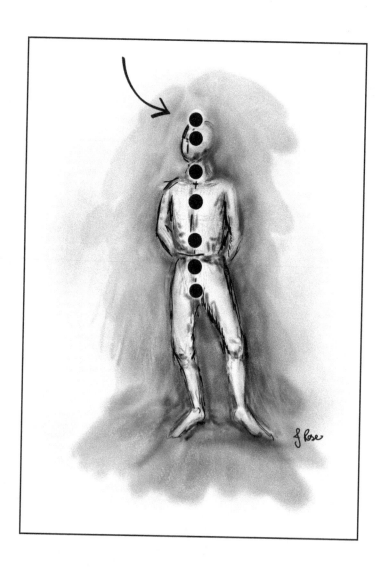

Chapter 8

The Seventh Chakra: The Crown Chakra— Our Connection to the Divine

Understanding this Energy

This energy is located at the top of the head. It is our connection to God, Great Spirit, the Divine, our higher power.

Certain acts, thoughts, and feelings can open us to connect to our higher power:

Our faith

Our dreams and inspirations of working for the greater good

Our ability to treat others kindly and respectfully

Our ability to have faith in God and trust in Divine timing

Being charitable

Honoring our personal values without offending, judging, or ridiculing others for not believing the same way

What Causes the Crown Chakra to Close and Block Energy?

The crown chakra's energies connect us to the Divine.

Tragedy and suffering are usually sudden, unexpected, and un-prepared for. A natural disaster such as an earthquake or hurricane can cause the crown chakra to close because we can't imagine how God could allow such devastation to occur.

Trauma can also happen over a longer period of time. Trauma is overwhelming and can leave a person feeling helpless, hopeless, and victimized. It is understandable why some people lose faith when they feel no one hears their cry for help.

Pain, whether acute or chronic, can change a person's outlook on life. It can alter the way we think, regardless of our faith. I used to take care of a lot of patients in the hospital with physical pain. That was something we frequently treated with narcotics, and many patients felt relief quickly. Psychological pain is not as easily relieved, particularly when our awareness is focused on finding ease. It can be challenging to connect to any energies beyond the self, whether it be God or even other people, when we are in distress.

Illness and suffering can either open or close the crown chakra. Some react to illness by blaming God when they are sick. Others have said their illness helped them deepen their connection to the Divine.

Grief is a pain like no other. We cannot escape the agony from grief if we have lived on this earth for any length of time. Grief can bring even the strongest individual down to his knees. I have felt grief at the deepest level of my soul, and it can also open or close the crown chakra. Some people blame God for taking their husband, their child, their pet. Others have said they felt God's presence through their journey through grief.

We can use negative, painful circumstances to deepen our connection to our faith. Yet we must be mindful not to judge others for how they handle these experiences. It is not our journey. All we can do is offer support, comfort, and connection. When you pray, remember to offer light and love to all the people you can think of who are suffering. Ask the Divine to create ease for them and that they feel His presence. It is a practice that will offer healing to others and to you.

The Physical or Psychological Effect of Blocked Energy at the Seventh Chakra

Chronic exhaustion that has no physical etiology. Have you ever slept for a long period of time and awakened feeling exhausted? Emotions have a vibrational frequency. Fear-based emotions, again, have a low vibration, which is why they feel heavy when they are stored in our body. Low and slow describe fear-based emotions, which make us feel tired even after we have slept all night. This includes feelings like humiliation, worthlessness, indecisiveness, inferiority, abandonment, hostility, anger, defensiveness, regret, jealousy, powerlessness, blame, betrayal, joylessness, loneliness, numbness/disconnectedness, worry, fear, doubt, hopelessness, frustration, bitterness, shame, rejection, heartache, guilt, insecurity.

Have you ever been around someone who was really negative, depressed, or severely anxious and felt like someone sucked the life right out of you? It can feel overwhelming and even exhausting. Yet listening to other people's problems is what I do. To avoid burnout, I practice blocking energy. An easy way to block energy is to imagine yourself in a bubble. You are still present, listening to someone intently, but the energy of the person is not getting absorbed into your body. Some negative energy still gets through because we are not robots, we are human beings. This is the reason why we feel exhausted after a long day at the office. This is also the reason why we must make time for balance.

When we are not connected spiritually, we feel exhausted and heavy. We fear death and the world becomes a dreadful place. We cannot feel hope, and we struggle to experience life as it is. We feel helpless and we feel hopeless. It can feel suffocating.

Extreme sensitivities to light and sound. Meditation, yoga, or Reiki can provide relief from these symptoms.

My story

The older I get, the more spiritual I feel. I owe a great deal of appreciation and gratitude to Deb Smith, a Native American Shaman, who helped me look outside the church to connect more deeply to God. I was referred to Deb Smith by a few different people. She lives in the town we used to live in, but is a spiritual advisor for many people from all over the world. I grew up Baptist and wasn't sure whether it was right to get advice from a spiritual advisor. I pushed through my hesitations and made an appointment. Before I arrived, I promised myself I would go in with an open mind, an open heart, and an open spirit.

Deb sees her clients out of a small house in Brooksville, Florida, a modest house to say the least. Deb told me to look for God in nature and in animals. She said if I didn't stay in the present, I might miss Him. The thought got me thinking and also noticing. Where do I see God, where do I see the Divine?

I see the Divine in the person who stops to hold the door open for me at the grocery store. I see the Divine when my husband gets called in the middle of the night by a sick patient, gets up, gets dressed, and heads to the hospital without complaining. I see the Divine when my neighbor offers to help me out with a difficult project around the house. I see the Divine in my children, my grandchildren, and the many children I work with in my office. I see the Divine in my husband when he looks at me with unconditional love. I see the Divine in my dog Henry, and I saw Him many times in Max. I feel the Divine working in me, and I look for the Divine in everyone I meet.

Case Study

I had a client who came to me to see me for counseling, wanting help with confidence and low self-worth. He was in his mid-thirties, handsome, and successful. He said he was happily married, and he and his wife had two young daughters. I remember wondering why he needed my help when he had everything he needed to be happy.

I saw this man for a few months and then received a random email from him that said, "My wife asked me to leave the house, and I am now living with my sister." He went on to say she had accused him of being abusive, and he had been admitted into a psychiatric facility because he had felt unstable. I read the email a few times and still couldn't make sense of it.

Over the next several months, their marital issues played out in court. It got uglier and uglier the longer it went on. He found himself in the middle of a divorce that had become so contentious, it was hard to imagine how he could recover.

I remember a session we had together. He came in, sat down, and said, "I am at the end of my rope." I didn't know what to say so we sat there together, in complete silence, for what seemed like hours. It was one of the most uncomfortable experiences I have ever had in therapy. When he finally spoke, he said, "I have lost faith in God. I have lost faith in everything I have ever believed in." I couldn't blame him. He was broken physically, mentally, and spiritually.

Eventually, their divorce was finalized and the client began dating again. He later told me about one night when he thought he couldn't go on to face another day. He was drowning in debt and had received another sizable bill from his attorney. Standing by his pool, he cried out to God and, suddenly, felt a sense of peace. He walked back inside, went to his computer, and noticed that a random deposit, an IRS refund he hadn't expected, had been made into his account. At that moment, he said he knew God was with him and that he would be okay.

How to Open the Crown Chakra

There are many things we can do for ourselves to raise our energetic vibrational frequency. It can be very difficult to let go of our ego and trust the Divine plan for our lives. This is the plan we may not understand, but it is essential for us to experience. My mother used to say, "Give it to God." Letting go of control, letting go of winning, letting go of the need to be right, letting go of getting the last word in, letting go of giving your opinion when it is not welcomed. I have learned to trust God and let go of a situation or a relationship when it is no longer working. Some people are meant to be in your life from beginning to end. Some people are meant to come into your life for a certain amount of time and then move on. Others come in, leave, and come back years later. Don't take it personally. Trust it.

I encourage my clients, and myself, to reframe negative feelings with higher-vibrational energies. Examples include willingness, hope, understanding, forgiveness, letting go, gratitude, serenity, joy, and love. These higher-frequency vibrations can keep us feeling happier, healthier, refreshed, and excited about life. A joyful person not only benefits himself, but every person he meets. Our energies have a ripple effect on everyone we come in contact with. It could be the cashier at the grocery store, our friends, our neighbors, our children, our spouses, even our pets. Honor yourself, do the work, stay balanced, and you can achieve and maintain these higher-vibrational energies with very little effort. Your perspective of every situation will determine your energies.

The Divine is not only teaching us but is also teaching others. We need to do our own work. We cannot learn lessons for other people. Many parents have a hard time watching their children struggle, which is why they swoop in and fix their problems for them. They pay the bills for their adult children, overstep boundaries, and cannot bear the thought of them failing. Worst-case scenarios are created to justify their behaviors and keep their children dependent on them. Did you know when a baby chick is pecking to get out of the shell, cracking the egg to help speed up the process will cause the baby chick to lack what it needs to survive? The time spent struggling and the tremendous work it takes for that baby chick to hatch is crucial. "Helping," in this case, does more harm than good. The same lesson is true for rescuing and enabling other people. We take away the lesson to be learned and prevent them from growing.

When we work to develop ourselves spiritually, our chakras will begin to open. We will develop trust in the Universe, trust God, trust that we are part of a Divine plan. We will let go of our ego more easily and connect to our higher power regularly. We will feel at peace and we will feel at ease. Results are frequently not immediate. Life is a marathon, not a sprint. I work diligently, regularly, on my path to spirituality. I hope you will too.

Words of Wisdom to Help Open the Seventh Chakra

Don't connect to a higher power
just when you want something.

Practice gratitude.

Resist giving problems to the Divine
and then taking them back.

Let go of your ego and trust the Divine.

Learn from children.

Stay present.

Look for the Divine in nature, in animals, and in each other.

Closing Thoughts

I have always felt connected to energy. I am intuitive, I receive messages, I have "God whispers," I sometimes predict things. I know I am connected to something greater than I, and to something farther than I can see. I receive signs, I have random thoughts I can't make sense of, I have déjà vu, I have strange dreams, animals communicate with me. It baffles my husband to no end. My clients tell me about their friends or relatives who have this physical ailment or a chronic condition. When I start to name the emotional issues attached to their problem, they say, "Is she your patient too?" I don't know the person to whom they are referring. I just understand the energy behind their physical condition.

I am grateful for this gift I have been blessed with but I also realize it comes with responsibility. For me, studying energy has helped me put all the pieces together. I see beyond what is. I have been blessed with knowledge and intuition. I trust it, I push through fear, I feel connected to God and the Universe. I am continually learning, and I accept life as it is even when it is painful. I struggle too.

I recognize the connection of body, mind, and spirit. It has rarely guided me in the wrong direction. I have learned to trust my instincts and listen to the body to communicate to me what it needs me to know. I hope you have learned enough to do your own work.

The truth is we can heal from within. We can improve our health by processing our thoughts, our perceptions, and our experiences. The body will follow the mind. Our thoughts and behaviors are contributing to our illnesses. I have seen it, I understand it, and I hope you will see it too.

My goal in writing this book was to help even one person find the courage to heal. In the Jewish Kabbalah there is a concept called Tikkun Olam, which means "heal the world." It may sound like a daunting task for one person, but if we all worked to touch the lives of just one person in a positive way, it could cause a ripple effect. If it kept going, we really could heal the world. Yogis hold their hands in prayer position and say "namaste," which means the light (of the Divine) in me sees and honors the light in you. What a wonderful message of hope.

There have been many books I have read that have helped me learn about physical, emotional, and spiritual energy. I have quoted Emily Maroutian's book, *The Energy of Emotions*, a few times writing this book. I also recommend her book, *The Book of Relief.*

Anatomy of the Spirit by Dr. Caroline Myss helped me understand the connection of emotional energy to physical well-being. Her insight provided a foundation for me. The Untethered Soul by Michael Singer helped me gain a better understanding of spiritual energy.

Iyanla Vanzant has written several books that have helped me with my personal journey. She had the courage to share her personal struggles in her writing, which helped me muster up enough strength to share mine.

Oprah Winfrey and Maya Angelou are individuals I have never met. I was sorry to learn of Maya Angelou's passing a few years ago. Yet we do not need to know each other physically to connect to each other's energies. I am thankful for their wisdom and guidance as both women have followed their dharma. I believe I am following mine too.

I am licensed nationally and in the state of Florida. Please visit my website at *deniseschonwald.com*. I look forward to hearing from you.

Epilogue

The Story of Max

We brought Max home in October 2005 after our children presented us with a PowerPoint presentation explaining why they felt they were responsible enough to take care of a dog. Our two daughters were twelve and fourteen and our son was nine at the time. Our son was ambivalent about taking care of a dog, but the girls were determined to persuade my husband to give in. They waited until he was fasting on Yom Kippur, hoping he was weak. This was their master plan. He gave in, and we bought the last dog in the litter, an apricot cockapoo.

Before we brought Max home, we all came up with a list of names. My husband wanted Brutus, but the girls were not about to allow it. We ended up having a family meeting over it and considered over twenty names. We decided on Max, after Miracle Max from The Princess Bride, only to find out later that Max is the most popular name for a dog.

Although we got Max for the children, he and I had a special bond. After practicing for a few years, I decided to share office space in my husband's office. He is a urologist and had plenty of room. It worked out perfectly. He was at one end of the office, and

Max and I were at the other. The staff did an excellent job managing both practices, and they were great about working in an office with a dog.

Before Max could join the practice, he had to pass a four-part test to become an official "therapy dog." He took his test at the same time our daughter, Lauren, was taking her CPA exam for accounting. Lauren passed the first part of her test, and Max passed his. Max passed the second part, and so did Lauren, and so on. Max was a natural and adapted to his new position with ease.

I put a dog door in my office and also on the door leading out to the waiting room so Max could have free roam. He loved it. He would fly in and out of the dog doors, and many of my husband's patients asked to schedule their next appointment on a day they knew Max would be in the office.

I frequently asked new clients why they chose me and the most consistent response was "you were the only counselor we could find who had a therapy dog." Max did not disappoint. He knew when to jump up on the sofa when clients were sad and when to lie on the floor and go to sleep when he was not needed. He knew when the session was due to end, right down to the minute, and would walk over and scratch the person on the leg. If they didn't get up, he'd jump up on the sofa and scratch again. If he was out and about in the office, he would come through the dog door. Patients would say, "I guess time is up," and start wrapping up their conversation. It was great.

Knowing Max was getting ready to turn fifteen, I decided to get another cockapoo, Henry, who came to us in November 2019. I figured Max might not want to practice with me for much longer or maybe he wouldn't be with me anymore, and I wanted to train his successor. I thought Henry would be a good fit.

Henry was spunky and full of life. There were many nights when Max would look at me with this blank stare as if to say, "What were you thinking?" because Henry was exhausting. I had moved my practice to Sarasota, and the change was quite an adjustment. I was glad I had Max with me for the transition.

Max was diagnosed with an aggressive cancer in April of 2020, and I could hardly stand the thought of parting with him. He declined over time and left us a few months later. I still miss him terribly.

I wanted to honor Max in a special way, and writing a book seemed fitting. I received kind words from over 200 people after Max passed away. Many knew him and his gift for helping people heal. My husband said he had quite the life, and we felt honored to have him as part of our family.

About Denise

In her thirty years working as a registered nurse within the ICU, Denise Schonwald cared for patients who were often in dire circumstances. She saw the patients and their families grappling with stress, anxiety, fear, and many other intense emotions. She, too, was affected by this challenging environment. In order to cope and help her patients cope, Denise learned various techniques to support mental and emotional well-being, in addition to taking care of the physical needs of a patient. Her success in striking a balance in treating the whole person led her to her calling as a licensed mental health counselor. By integrating mental health and physical health into a cohesive treatment plan, Denise provides a more holistic approach to her patients.

Denise has expertise in helping clients through a variety of mental and emotional struggles, including marital strife, adolescent behavior issues, familial relationship issues, childhood trauma, and more. To assist her in the practice, Denise worked with Max, her therapy dog, for many years before his passing in June of 2020. Henry, a rambunctious apricot cockapoo, is a recent addition to the practice and is currently in training. We are confident he will continue Max's legacy and provide love and healing to many.

Additional sources of inspiration for Denise include physical activity and various forms of meditation, which help relieve stress and provide mental clarity. Denise enjoys yoga and competitive tennis, balancing the physical exercise with meditation, Reiki, and aromatherapy for mental and emotional well-being. Understanding the connection between the mind, body, and spirit, Denise helps clients to explore each avenue, to achieve their own optimum level of health and wellness.

My hope is that you do the work, love your life, and live in peace, good health, and happiness.

Namaste,
Denise

Index